THE FIRST MUSIC TEACHER

THE FIRST MUSIC TEACHER

How to Raise a Musical Child Without Lessons, Talent, or Even a Perfect Voice

Adrian Edward

Copyright © 2026 Adrian Edward

All rights reserved. No part of this publication may be reproduced, distributed, or transmitted in any form or by any means, including photocopying, recording, or other electronic or mechanical methods, without the prior written permission of the publisher, except in the case of brief quotations embodied in critical reviews and certain other noncommercial uses permitted by copyright law. For permission requests, write to the publisher, addressed "Attention: Permissions Coordinator," at the address below.

ISBN: 979-8-9892244-2-5 (Paperback)

Any references to historical events, real people, or real places may have been changed to protect individual privacy.

Book cover design by Katarina.

Printed in the United States of America.

First printing edition 2026.

CMM Press
Hampstead, NC

www.TheFirstMusicTeacher.com

"The first music a child hears is their parent's voice. Everything else is just harmony."

-Adrian Edward

Contents

Part IV

From Sound to Symbols

Conclusion

Carrying the Music Forward

Appendix

Resources and Activities

Foreword

If you're a parent curious about early childhood music education, you're holding the right book. I wish I'd had this guide to motivate me and boost my confidence when I began homeschooling my six children years ago.

Some of my fondest childhood memories are of playing the piano and singing with my mother. I wanted my children to share that joy, but the music myths Adrian describes in these pages held me back.

Because I lacked confidence in my piano skills, I believed I couldn't teach my kids. So, I hired a talented piano teacher. She played beautifully but soon grew frustrated with my younger son's immaturity and recommended delaying his music instruction. This reinforced my misconception that a child must be "old enough" to learn music or even that they shouldn't start until they can be "good" at it.

I didn't apply this logic to other childhood activities. I'd never withhold art supplies or sports equipment until my children were "good" at painting or soccer. Yet, my husband and I fell for another music myth that also shaped our approach to art and sports: the belief that children are either born with talent or they aren't.

While the most gifted musicians may have innate traits that contribute to their greatness, not every child needs to be a prodigy. They may not become legendary musicians or earn millions from their music, and they don't have to.

A homeschooling friend once shared, "I was told I couldn't sing and even though I loved singing, I stopped." That breaks my heart. Music instruction can simply be for a child's enjoyment and for yours as their parent. The benefits don't depend on being "good" at it.

Another myth that hindered our music education was the fear of becoming an overzealous "music police" parent. I knew a homeschool mom obsessed with her son's music practice, and I vowed not to be like her. I'd rather let my child quit music than push too hard. But, as Adrian explains, I wouldn't take that approach with language. As a writer and speaker, I'd never consider abandoning language development. Instead, I'd engage my child with diverse formats and approaches. We can do the same with music.

As a busy mom, I didn't know how to provide my young children with a music education beyond piano lessons, and I lacked the time to research and create a plan. If you can relate, you'll love this handbook for becoming your child's first music teacher.

Adrian shares his own inspiring story of learning music and language, provides research on music's impact on developing brains, and offers easy-to-implement activities for teaching.

I had the pleasure of meeting Adrian and his wife at a homeschool conference. He embodies everything you'd want in a music teacher: kindness, passion, and fun. While Adrian can't come to your home, this book brings his expertise to you.

By following these pages, you'll become the kind, passionate, and fun music teacher your children need and will fondly remember.

Melanie Wilson, Ph.D.
Psychologist and author of *Grammar Galaxy* and *Training Aliens* curricula

A Note to the Reader

This book is your guide to bringing music into your home, *without stress or pressure.*

You'll discover why every parent can teach music, how children naturally absorb it as a language, and simple ways to turn everyday moments into joyful lessons.

Read it one chapter at a time, or skip to what feels most relevant —**you already have what it takes to make music part of your family's life**.

Introduction

My Story

> *Every child can learn the language of music. The question is not whether they will learn, but what they will learn about themselves in the process.*
>
> -Leonard Bernstein

When I was in high school, I faced what seemed like an insignificant decision. To complete my elective credits for graduation, I had to choose between an art class and a music class. Little did I know this "small" choice would change the course of my life.

My father was a remarkably talented painter, and I grew up watching him create hundreds of paintings. While I enjoyed dabbling in painting and could appreciate everything from Picasso to Monet, my passion for the visual arts didn't run as deep as his. I admired and loved his enthusiasm, but I didn't connect with it in the same way. So, art class was out, leaving music as my only option.

The problem? I was, frankly, the least musical person you could imagine. My teenage world revolved around skateboarding, movies, and video games, not exactly a résumé I'm proud of, but I'll claim the "young and naive" pass.

Growing up, we had a piano at home, but it served more as a shelf for knick-knacks than an instrument for music. I had no strong feelings about music one way or another.

With only two choices before me, I circled music, set my schedule, and showed up to my first music class with zero expectations. Our teacher, Mr. Rubin, arrived a few minutes late, sat at the piano, and began playing "The Star-Spangled Banner." It was impressive. I was fascinated by how two hands could coax so much sound from a single instrument and it might have been the first time I truly heard a piano played.

Then he played it again. "Okay, this is weird," I thought. And again. And again. My classmates and I exchanged confused glances. After the fifth round, one friend shrugged, stood up, and walked out. "Bold move," I thought, half-expecting no end to this loop. But as he left, the piano stopped. A wave of relief swept the room.

Mr. Rubin finally spoke: "That's fascinating, students usually leave by the third round!" He had, in today's terms, trolled us. Well played, Mr. Rubin. That quirky introduction hooked me. There was something captivating about the sounds I heard coming from the piano that day, and I wanted to learn how to make them myself.

That decision altered my life in countless ways, inspiring even the words you're reading now. Music was clearly something special, and I wanted in, whatever that meant.

My Bilingual Life at Home

I grew up in a loving family that spoke two languages. My parents spoke to me in Spanish, while I used English with my sisters and friends at school. Looking back, I didn't fully appreciate the gift of bilingualism until much later. It was just part of life. Didn't everyone speak two languages at home?

My daily routine was predictable. At school, I spoke, read, and wrote in English. At home, I watched TV and chatted with my sisters in English. But with my parents, it was Spanish, exclusively. No "Spanglish" or mixing languages in our household. This created a clear distinction between the two, and remarkably, there was never any confusion.

If you're wondering whether learning multiple languages as a child causes confusion, research shows children can learn up to four languages without issue. We often underestimate the power of young minds, something to consider if you want your kids to be multilingual. Today, I'm fluent in both Spanish and English, able to express complex thoughts in either language. I love choosing whether to read a book in English or Spanish.

Being bilingual feels like a "superpower" that opens up the world. What's more, I never formally studied Spanish, it came naturally from speaking with my parents. I later applied the

English grammar I learned in school to Spanish, enabling me to read and write it fluently. Those early years learning Spanish set the stage for a lifetime of learning.

My Aha! Moment

As I progressed in high school music class, I was amazed at how naturally music came together. Learning to read, write, and play felt intuitive, despite it being a completely new "language" I'd never encountered. Why was I picking it up so quickly?

I'd love to claim some prodigious talent, but the truth is, there was nothing inherently special about me. What *was* special was my environment. Years into my music teaching career, I noticed patterns in my students. Those exposed to music in their earliest years grasped rhythms, nuances, and the language of music more easily. Students with little early exposure struggled more.

Then it hit me: though I hadn't been exposed to much music as a child, I *had* learned Spanish fluently. Music, I realized, is another language and my bilingual brain was wired to learn it more easily.

My bilingual upbringing fostered a growth mindset. Deep down, I believed learning something new wasn't daunting; it just required effort and time. Learning Spanish became a blueprint for tackling future challenges, including music.

This realization convinced me that early education opens new channels of learning for every child. Specifically, learning a second language, or even music, is not just possible but natural at a young age.

Why I Wrote This Book

As a preschool music teacher in Brooklyn and later at the Collegiate School in New York City, I had the joy of teaching thousands of students. I'm forever grateful to leaders like Alice Guercio and Don Sorel, who gave me the freedom to expand the curriculum as I saw fit.

I'm a firm believer that humans excel at learning with clear direction and time. I also believe we all learn differently, so keeping education fun and varied is essential to avoid rigid, uninspiring experiences. With this philosophy and the green light from my leaders, I aimed to provide every student, no matter how young, with a true music education, one where they'd learn to listen, read, write, play, and create music.

If you recall preschool or kindergarten, you likely remember singing and maybe dancing, but not much actual music education. There were probably shakers but no instruments like pianos or melodic tools, and certainly no focus on playing discernible melodies. Most early music curricula emphasize listening, singing along, or simple movements to songs like "Hokey Pokey" or "Itsy Bitsy Spider." These are wonderful foundations, but they fall short of teaching music when children are more than capable of learning it.

Too often, people believe young children are too busy learning their native language to tackle another, like music. Oh, how wrong that is! Children are wired to learn multiple languages. In the chapters ahead, I'll show you, with scientific evidence, how a child's brain is perfectly suited for language learning and how we've underestimated young minds for too long. Perhaps you've underestimated them, too.

I wrote this book to show you, as a parent, that your child can thrive in early music education. With my Color Me Mozart curriculum, it's so simple that you can, and will be their best teacher.

How This Book Will Benefit You

Nobel laureate Eric Kandel said, "Learning a new language is learning a new way to think about the world, and this reshapes the brain itself."

As someone passionate about learning and embracing new challenges, I believe each new skill deepens our appreciation of the world. One of the most valuable skills we carry is the ability to communicate through language, written and spoken. These very words are a testament to that.

Music was a gift I didn't know I needed. It was like unmuting the soundtrack of my life. Before that high school music class, I hadn't realized music was missing—it was just background noise in movies or on the radio. That fateful day changed everything. I want that for you and your family, without waiting for a high school elective.

In the following pages, I'll show you how to be your child's first and most influential music teacher, even if you've never studied music or think you lack the skills. I'll guide you to become your own first music teacher, too. How's that for flipping music education on its head?

To get there, we'll explore how our brains process language and the science behind it. While we'll dive into the research, I'll also provide a practical, step-by-step plan, grounded in neuroscience, education, and my years of teaching, to bring fun, accessible music education into your home with you as the teacher.

I'll break down language and music learning into their smallest parts, making them easy to understand and mirroring how we naturally learn language. I know you may have heard that music requires innate talent, a "good ear," or a special gift.
I'm here to tell you those ideas are outdated and misguided. Need proof you and your child can learn music together? Consider this: by age three, you knew about 1,000 words before you could even read. How did that happen?

Let's find out.

Part I

Why You (Yes, You) Can Teach Music

Chapter 1

Smash the Myth: Music is Only for the "Gifted"

> *Music is not a luxury for the talented few, it's a language every child deserves to speak.*
>
> -Adrian Edward

I'll never forget the first time someone told me music was a gift, a talent you either had or didn't. The message was clear: music belonged to the chosen few. If you weren't born with it, you might as well step aside and let the "talented" kids take the stage.

This idea clashed with what I felt deep down, especially given my fluency in Spanish alongside English. For years, I wrestled with whether talent was inherited or developed. After teaching thousands of music students, I reached a clear conclusion: music isn't about talent, it's about access. I was looking at the question all wrong. What it's really about is giving children the same opportunities with music as we give them with language, movement, or play. When it comes to music or any developmental area in a child's life, we must confront the myths we've been led to believe. One pervasive myth, that music is only for the "gifted" or "musical" child, stops many parents from encouraging their kids to explore music.

Sadly, this mindset isn't just limited to music; we apply it to other subjects, too. I've met countless parents who claim they're "tone-deaf" or can't keep a beat. And I'm not immune from this type of thinking either. Growing up, I'd say things like, "I'm not good at math" or "history isn't my thing." I believed those thoughts to be so true that I would often stop trying altogether, making it a self-fulfilling prophecy.

To be clear, I'm not suggesting we must love every subject. But claiming we're "not good" at something just because it doesn't come naturally is misguided and sets a dangerous precedent for our children.

The neuroscientist, musician, and author, Daniel Levitin, puts it this way:

> *Even just a small exposure to music lessons as a child creates neural circuits for music processing that are enhanced and more efficient than for those who lack training"*

Levitin goes on to discuss how even brief childhood music training has lasting neural benefits, countering the idea that lessons "don't take" if someone doesn't become a professional.

Consider the words you're reading right now. As I write and you read, you're not only understanding each individual word and sentence but you're also grasping the ideas embedded in each paragraph. That alone is miraculous. How can your brain process so much information at once? And yet it does.

Even more astonishing is that by age five, a child typically learns about 3,500 words annually, absorbing language effortlessly from their environment. We don't call that "talent", we call it learning.

Music Is a Language — Not a Talent

LANGUAGE	MUSIC
AGE 0–1 YRS Babbling → First words "Da-da"	**AGE 0–1 YRS** Cooing → First hums/claps Hums to lullaby
AGE 1–3 YRS 50-1,000 Words Simple sentences	**AGE 1–3 YRS** Echoes rhythms, sings bits "Twinkle" with gestures
AGE 3–5 YRS ~3,500 new words/year Full conversations	**AGE 3–5 YRS** Matches pitch, invents songs Full nursery rhymes

If your child learned thousands of words before ever stepping into a classroom or beginning a formal education, imagine what else their young mind can absorb when given the chance. You're not "bad" at math, history, or music, you simply haven't had the opportunity to learn it in a natural, immersive way, like you did with language. Music is not about becoming a virtuoso; it's about opening a door to a new way of thinking and connecting.

■ Did You Know?

Music Boosts Early Development
A 2015 study found that children as young as three who engage in simple music activities (like clapping rhythms or singing) show improved language skills, memory, and emotional regulation, regardless of "natural talent" (Williams et al., 2015). Music is for everyone!

Your Child's Most Influential Teacher: You

Let's start with perhaps not so obvious but powerful truth: you are your child's first and most influential music teacher. Long before any private lessons or music class, your musical influence shapes their world. The way you sing with them, dance with them, clap rhythms, or hum while cooking dinner, it all matters.

> *When a child absorbs language effortlessly from their environment, we don't call that "talent", we call it learning.*

Think about how children learn language. They don't learn to speak from a textbook; they learn from the adults around them. If not for parents, family, or friends talking to them, they'd never master their native language. Yet many parents instinctively feel unqualified to teach music, assuming it requires a certain expertise they lack.

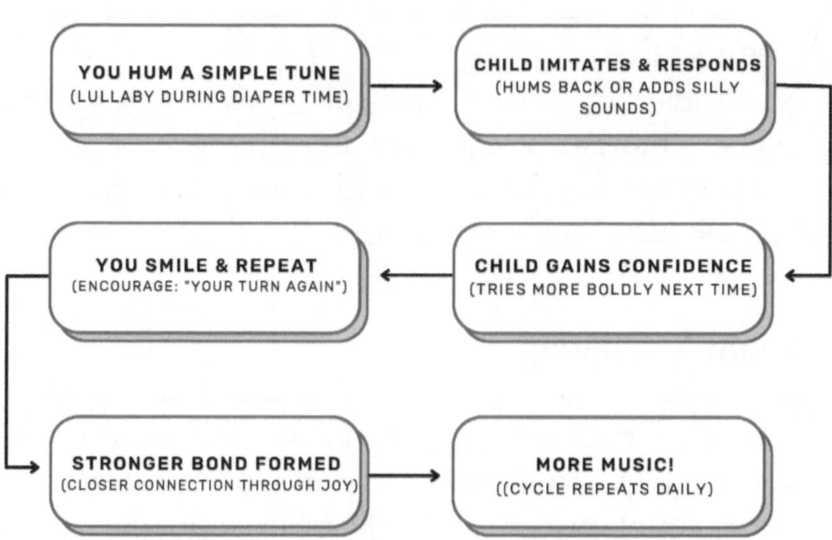

Here's a revealing thought: most parents don't have PhDs in English literature, yet they teach their kids grammar, pronunciation, and vocabulary every day. It's not about credentials, it's about an innate ability to teach and pass on information which you already possess.

From day one, your voice is the one your child hears and responds to most. You never doubted your ability to teach your child their first words or letters, you just did it. You surrounded them with age-appropriate toys, games, and books, offering knowledge in bite-sized chunks. And just as you cut food small enough for them to chew, you can introduce music in simple, digestible ways that build fluency and spark joy.

■ Try This at Home

Daily Hum-Along
Hum a simple tune (e.g., a lullaby or jingle) during routines like diaper changes or car rides. Encourage your child to hum back or add sounds. This builds imitation and confidence, like teaching first words.

■ Parent Takeaway

You don't need to be a musician to teach music. Your encouragement and presence are enough to make music a natural part of your child's life, just like language.

Music is a Language, Not a Performance

Children learn to speak by babbling, trying, and making mistakes. We don't wait for perfect pronunciation before encouraging them to talk. Music works the same way. It's not about performing for an audience, it's about fluency, exploration, and expression without fear of failure.

Too often, music education is framed as merely preparation for recitals or competitions. But that misses the bigger picture.

We don't teach kids to speak just so they can become actors; we teach them to speak so they connect with the world, express their ideas, and live fully. Music offers the same gift.

According to Collins Dictionary, a *language* is "a system of communication using sounds and symbols." That's precisely what music is, an avenue for communication and expression, not a skill exclusively reserved for the stage.

Consider your own experience learning language. In your first few years, you mastered sounds and words, then connected them to written symbols, all prior to formal training. Your brain, guided by the people around you, was perfectly suited to make sense of all of the input it received and transform it into language. Music follows this same learning path. A child's brain is built to learn languages, including music, through immersion and play.

Many parents tell me their kids stopped music lessons because they felt "pressure" to perform. That's a sign music was taught as a skill to master, not a language to speak. We don't stop teaching kids to read or write because they struggle with their first words. We encourage every syllable and celebrate every step. Music deserves the same patience. It's not about perfection, it's about expanding your child's ability to express themselves, deepening their appreciation of the world, and boosting cognitive skills that benefit every area of life.

My Journey to Redefining Music Education

As a musician and later an educator, I saw a different reality. Time and again, I watched children light up through music, whether or not anyone called them "talented." What mattered was opportunity, encouragement, and joy, not so-called natural ability. Music education isn't a luxury; it's a foundation. As science continues to prove, music stimulates a large portion of children's brains while developing things such as focus, empathy, coordination, and language skills.

Most importantly, it strengthens the bond between parent and child. This realization reshaped how I teach music and how I view learning as a whole. It inspired me to create my Color Me Mozart curriculum, which makes music education accessible to every child and parent, no matter their musical background.

■ Did You Know?

Music Builds Empathy

2013 study found that shared music activities foster empathy and social bonds in young children, enhancing emotional intelligence (Rabinowitch et al., 2013). Music connects us!

■ Try This at Home

Sound Safari
Take your child on a "sound safari" around the house. Tap a spoon on a pot, shake a box of cereal, or hum a tune. Have them mimic the sounds or create their own. Ask, "What does this sound make you think of?" This builds listening skills, creativity, and confidence in making music, showing it's as natural as talking.

■ Parent Takeaway

Treat music like babbling, encourage every sound. It's expression, not performance, building fluency without pressure.

■ Chapter Recap

1. **Music isn't just for the "gifted."**
   Talent is a myth, anyone can learn music with opportunity and practice, just like learning to speak.
2. **You're your child's best music teacher.**
   Your encouragement and presence make you the most influential guide, no musical expertise needed.
3. **Music is a language, not a performance.**
   Like speaking, music is about expression and connection, not perfect recitals.
4. **Simple activities build fluency.**
   Clapping rhythms or exploring sounds helps kids learn music naturally, like they learn words.

Part II

The Parent-as-Teacher Mindset

Chapter 2

You Already Have What It Takes

> *Music expresses that which cannot be said and on which it is impossible to be silent.*

-Victor Hugo

When I first laid eyes on sheet music in that piano class, it was like discovering a secret code. Those curious black dots, lines, and symbols on the page seemed to hold a kind of magic.

I couldn't explain why I was so drawn to it, but I felt an instant connection. Then, during my first few piano lessons, I watched those two-dimensional symbols transform into something extraordinary, melodies and harmonies that could make my heart soar or bring tears to my eyes. It was as if the music was speaking a language I'd always known but hadn't yet learned to articulate.

As I fell deeper in love with music, I began to wonder: Where did this passion come from? Why was I so captivated by rhythm, melody, and harmony? The answer, I realized, was all around me. Music had been woven into the fabric of my life long before I ever touched a piano. Bass virtuoso Victor Wooten puts it perfectly in *The Music Lesson*:

> *"I'm just comparing the two languages (English and Music) and your processes of learning them. If Music and English are both languages, then why not apply the process used to get good at one of them to the other?" (Wooten, 2006, p. 5)*

That's exactly what happened for me. My fluency in Spanish alongside English made music feel like just another dialect waiting to be spoken. No wonder it clicked so fast. Even though we didn't grow up listening to much music in our house, when I begin to reminisce, I do remember my father playing a fair amount to inspire his painting. Back then, there were no digital formats or even CDs. He listened on eight-tracks, those chunky cassettes with visible reels.

My dad's collection was eclectic to say the least, ranging from Argentine tangos to blues greats like Muddy Waters and, of course, the legendary Bob Marley. Looking back, I didn't know any friend's dad with such a varied selection at the time.

In contrast, at school I sang nursery rhymes like *Twinkle, Twinkle, Little Star* in kindergarten with my classmates. We even put on the occasional play featuring hits from that era. And the cartoons I watched on TV? They came with catchy jingles and sweeping soundtracks that stuck in my head. Music was everywhere, shaping me in ways I didn't even notice at the time.

But could this early exposure to music really have made such a profound impact on my life? The answer, it turns out, is a resounding yes. Science backs this up in fascinating ways. Neuroscientists Susan Rogers and Ogi Ogas, in their book *This Is What It Sounds Like*, explain that our connection to music begins even before we're born:

> *"In the final trimester of pregnancy, the auditory system is developed enough that muffled sounds reach the baby. The brain at this stage can process simple melodic patterns, like the intonations of a mother's voice, which is why newborns prefer its familiar sound over an unfamiliar voice."*

When I first read this, I was floored. The idea that we're absorbing music *in the womb* seemed almost too incredible to believe. But the more I learned about how infants process sound, the more it made sense. Think about it: a baby can actually hear their mother's voice, her heartbeat, the rhythm of her breathing. These sounds aren't just background noise, they're the first music

Your child's first music lesson starts before birth.

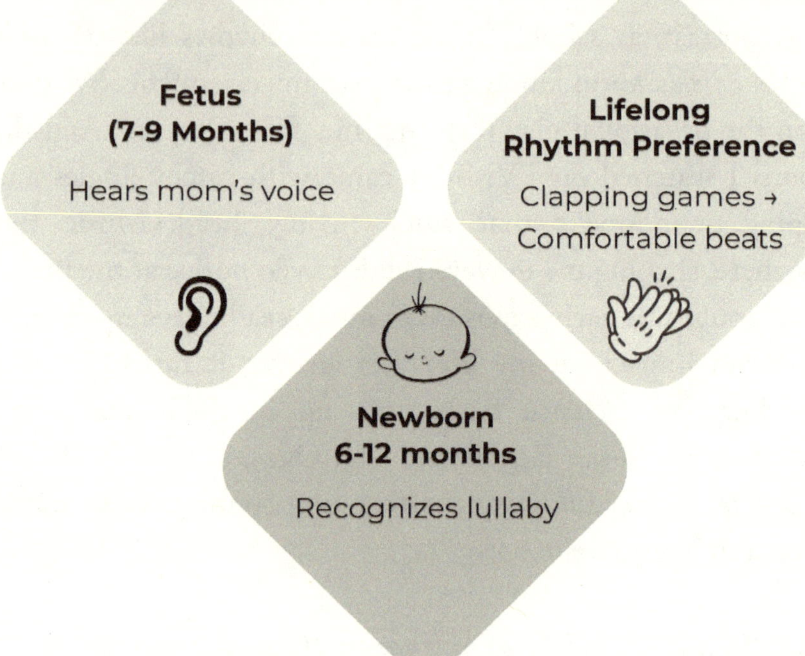

a child experiences, wiring their brain to recognize patterns and rhythms from the very start.

This early connection to sound doesn't stop at birth. Rhythm, in particular, plays a powerful role in shaping us. In his book *Musicophilia*, neuroscientist Oliver Sacks notes:

> *"The rhythms we hear in the first year of life, especially from 6 to 12 months old, become the rhythms we feel most comfortable with for the rest of our lives."*

This blew my mind. This meant that the lullabies my mother sang, the steady beats coming out my dad's eight-track player while he painted, and even the playful clapping games I played in school, they weren't just fleeting, inconsequential moments. They were embedding themselves in my brain, shaping how I connect with music today. And I bet you can relate.

Maybe there's a song from your childhood, a lullaby your parent sang, a jingle from a favorite show, or a nursery rhyme from preschool, that instantly transports you back.

You don't just hear the music; you *feel* it. The emotions, the smells, the memories come flooding back, as vivid as if they happened yesterday.

This is the power of music. It creates neural pathways that run deep, linking sounds to emotions, memories, and moments in our lives. For children, this makes music more than just a fun activity, it's a cornerstone of their development. And here's the exciting part: you, as a parent, are already equipped to tap into this natural connection and nurture it in your child.

By building on the music that's already part of their world, those lullabies, nursery rhymes, or even the silly songs you make up together, you can help them become fluent in the language of music, just as they become fluent in spoken language.

■ Did You Know?

Music Boosts Memory from Day One

Babies as young as a few months old recognize melodies heard in the womb. A 2014 study found stronger neural responses to familiar lullabies (Hepper et al., 2014). Your voice is their first music lesson!

You Teach Your Child to Talk, Why Not Music Too?

As I've traveled the country speaking at conferences and meeting parents, I've heard one concern over and over: "I'd love to teach my child music, but I'm not qualified." Many parents assume they need to be musicians themselves or have years of formal training to teach their kids music.

I get it.

With all the social media posts of virtuosic musicians and intimidating music teachers out there, it's easy to feel like music education is best left to the "experts." But I'm here to tell you: you *are* qualified. In fact, you're the *best* person to be your child's first music teacher.

Let's flip the script and think about this differently. When you teach your child to talk, do you worry about not being a linguist? Of course not! You don't need a degree in linguistics to help your toddler say "mama" or "dada." You start with simple words, repeat them lovingly, and celebrate every babble and attempt.

Over time, those small moments add up, and your child builds a vocabulary, learns to form sentences, and eventually tells stories. Music works the same way. You don't need to know music theory or play an instrument to teach your child the building blocks of music, rhythm, melody, and movement.

Let's break it down by comparing music to language, something you're already an expert at teaching your child. When you teach your toddler to speak, you don't start with Shakespeare or complex grammar rules. You begin with simple, digestible words like "ball," "dog," or "milk."

You sing songs like "Itsy Bitsy Spider," using gestures to make it fun and memorable. You read picture books with rhyming text, keeping the language engaging and age-appropriate. The goal isn't to overwhelm your child with advanced vocabulary; it's to spark curiosity and build a foundation they can grow from.

Same method. Same joy. No degree required.

LANGUAGE	MUSIC
Say "mama" → Repeat → Celebrate	Hum lullaby → Echo → Giggle
Read rhyming books	Sing "Itsy Bitsy" with gestures
Count toys → "1, 2, 3"	Clap rhythm → "clap-clap-pause

Music education for young children follows the same principle. You don't need to teach your three-year-old how to read sheet music or play a Beethoven sonata. Instead, you start with the basics: clapping a rhythm, singing a simple melody, or moving to the beat of a song.

These are the "ABCs" of music, and they're as easy to teach as the alphabet. For example, when you clap along to "Twinkle, Twinkle, Little Star" or make up a silly song about brushing teeth, you're teaching your child rhythm and melody without even realizing it. These small, joyful moments lay the groundwork for a lifelong love of music.

Proof You Don't Need to Know Music (The Grant Family, Texas)

Lucy and Jeff have three kids and exactly zero musical training between them.

Yet on winter mornings their house turns into a music studio: 12-year-old Maya at the guitar working through anxiety, 10-year-old Michael finally brave enough to try, and 8-year-old Molly playing piano and singing backup.

Sometimes the "school day" begins later than usual because the kids have already spent hours creating songs together. Luciana wrote: "I used to worry we weren't doing enough. Now I know one of the best gifts we could give our children was music in our home. It brings us all together in such a special way and helps the kids focus on every other subject."

If a formerly musically "untrained" mom and dad in Texas can raise kids who breathe music, your living room is already more than qualified. Just like early language, all you need to do is put it out there for your kids to absorb. Give them the tools to express themselves through music, and in the process, learn music with them.

It's one of the strongest "permission slips" you can give them.

■ Did You Know?

Rhythm Is Universal

Seven-month-olds detect rhythmic patterns across cultures (Hannon & Trehub, 2019). Your child is born ready!

Here's where we've gone astray with music education. Somewhere along the way, we started treating music like an elite skill, reserved for professionals or those with "natural talent." A century ago, music was a family affair, parents sang folk songs, grandparents played simple instruments, and communities gathered to make music together.

But today, we've outsourced music education to specialists, leaving many parents feeling like they don't have what it takes. I'm here to say: you *do*. Just as you teach your child to count before they learn algebra, you can teach them the basics of music before they ever step into a formal lesson.

Think about math for a moment. Even if you're not a mathematician, you probably taught your child to recognize numbers or count to ten. You might have played games like "How many apples are in the basket?" or counted steps as you climbed the stairs together. These simple activities gave your child a foundation that made math class easier later on.

Music is no different.

By introducing your child to rhythm through clapping games, melody through singing, or movement through dancing, you're giving them a head start. When they eventually take lessons or join a choir, they'll already have a sense of music's building blocks, making the experience richer and more rewarding.

The best part? Teaching your child music isn't just about preparing them for future lessons, it's about creating moments of connection with you. When you sing a lullaby, clap a rhythm, or dance together in the living room, you're not just teaching music; you're building memories.

These shared experiences strengthen your bond and show your child that music is a joyful, natural part of life. Unlike formal lessons, which often focus on technique, your role as their first music teacher is about fostering curiosity, confidence, and love for music.

■ Try This at Home

Copycat Rhythm Game

Putting It Into Practice

So, how do you start? It's simpler than you think. At Color Me Mozart, we've created an entire music curriculum and designed tools to make music education accessible for parents, no matter your background. The curriculum breaks music down into bite-sized, playful activities that fit into your daily routine.

But you don't need a full curriculum to begin with music education from day one. For example, try this: next time you're in the car, sing a favorite nursery rhyme and clap the rhythm together. Or make up a silly song about breakfast while you're cooking. These moments don't require sheet music or an instrument, they just require you and your child having fun together.

■ Did You Know?

Music Builds Empathy
Group music activities increase cooperation and emotional understanding in young children (Kirschner & Tomasello, 2016). Shared songs wire hearts together!

■ Parent Takeaway

You teach language without a degree—do the same with music. Simple, repeated play builds fluency and bonds.

Here's a quick activity to try today: Play a "copycat" rhythm game. Clap a simple pattern (like *clap-clap-pause-clap*), and ask your child to copy it. Then let them create a rhythm for you to copy. Add silly sounds or movements to keep it fun, maybe stomp your feet or tap the table. This game teaches rhythm, builds listening skills, and sparks creativity, all while making your child giggle. (And yes, giggling is a key part of the process!)

The beauty of this approach is that it mirrors how you teach language. You don't expect your child to speak in full sentences right away; you celebrate their first words and build from there. With music, celebrate their first claps, their first sung notes, their first dance moves. Every small step is wiring their brain for learning, creativity, and emotional connection.

As you embark on this journey, remember that you're not just teaching music, you're giving your child a gift that will enrich their life. Music fluency, like language fluency, opens doors to self-expression, confidence, and joy. And the best part? You get to be there for every note, every rhythm, every moment of discovery.

By embracing your role as your child's first music teacher, you're not just teaching them music, you're unlocking a world of creativity, connection, and lifelong learning. So, turn up the music, grab your child's hands, and start this journey together. You've got this!

■ Did You Know?

Music Boosts Language
Music activities improve vocabulary and reading in children (Gordon et al., 2014). Singing rhythms supercharges speech!

■ Try This at Home

Silly Song Breakfast
Make up a tune about your morning routine (e.g., "Pancakes flipping, syrup dripping"). Sing it together while eating. This weaves melody into daily life, like rhyming books for words.

■ Parent Takeaway

Start small and celebrate every sound. You're already your child's expert, music is just another way to connect.

■ Chapter Recap

1. **Music Is in You Already**: From the womb to your childhood, music has shaped who you are. Your child is wired to connect with music, and you're the perfect person to guide them.
2. **You Don't Need to Be an Expert**: Just as you teach your child to speak or count, you can teach them the basics of music, rhythm, melody, and movement, without any formal training.
3. **Keep It Simple and Fun**: Start with playful activities like clapping rhythms or singing nursery rhymes. These small moments build a foundation for a lifelong love of music.
4. **Connection Is the Key**: Teaching your child music isn't just about skills, it's about creating joyful, shared experiences that strengthen your bond.

Chapter 3

The Real Purpose of Early Music Education

> *I would teach children music, physics, and philosophy; but most importantly music, for in the patterns of music and all the arts are the keys of learning.*
>
> -Plato, *The Republic*

When I think back to my childhood, even though I didn't know it at the time or even play an instrument, music was all around me, from the cartoons I watched to the silly jingles from TV commercials. As I grew older, began studying music, and eventually became a music educator, I realized that music does so much more than entertain; it's a powerful tool for unlocking a child's potential in ways that ripple far beyond the notes.

You might already sense that music, like many activities, teaches skills that go beyond the activity itself. To illustrate this, let's compare music to something that's familiar to all of us: sports. Growing up, I loved soccer (or *fútbol*, as we called it in Spanish). I still have great memories of my first years learning to play. It took years to learn how to dribble, pass, and shoot effectively. But soccer wasn't just about kicking a ball; it taught me teamwork, persistence, and the value of showing up even when I was tired.

Music teaches life skills, just like sports.

MUSIC
Clap rhythm → Focus
Sing together → Empathy
Retry tricky note → Grit

LANGUAGE
Dribble ball → Coordination
Pass to teammate → Teamwork
Miss shot, try again → Resilience

Whether your favorite sport is basketball, swimming, or something else, you've likely experienced this too. Think about a time you played a sport or watched your child on a team. Beyond the physical skills, like shooting a basket or swinging a bat, there were deeper lessons: discipline, patience, grit, and the joy of working together toward a goal.

Music works exactly the same way. It's not just about playing notes or singing songs; it's about building a foundation for life.

Early music education lights up a child's brain, strengthens their body, and deepens their emotional connections. And the best part? You, as a parent, can guide your child through this journey, just as you cheer them on in sports or help them with their first words.

This was at the heart of my dream for Color Me Mozart: to show you how to make music a fun, natural part of your child's life, unlocking benefits that will stay with them forever.

■ Did You Know?

Music Lights Up the Whole Brain
Music activities engage auditory, motor, and emotional brain regions at once, creating cross-brain connections (Zatorre, 2016). Music is a supercharger!

Lessons Beyond the Notes

Let's dive deeper into the sports comparison. In soccer, I had to learn the basics: how to control the ball, pass to a teammate, or aim for the goal. Without those skills, I wouldn't have been much use on the field, and honestly, it wouldn't have been all that fun.

But the real magic of sports happened off the field. Whenever I missed a shot on goal and my teammates encouraged me to try again, I learned resilience. When we strategized together, I learned collaboration. When we lost a game and then showed up to our next game, I learned grit. These lessons shaped who I am today, in my relationships, my work, and even how I approach challenges as a parent and educator.

Fun fact: I still love playing soccer, and the life lessons I learned early on are still with me to this day. Music offers the same kind of transformative lessons in a child's life. When your child claps a rhythm or sings a song, they're not just learning music; they're developing focus, coordination, and emotional intelligence.

For example, when you play a simple clapping game together, your child practices listening carefully (auditory processing), moving in time (motor skills), and taking turns (empathy). These skills translate to the classroom and homeschool settings, where focus helps with math, or to friendships, where empathy builds trust. Music, like sports, is a vehicle for growth, and you don't need to be a professional musician to make it happen.

> ***Here's the key:*** *the goal of early music education isn't to create the next Mozart or pop star. Just as we don't teach kids to read so they can become best-selling novelists, we don't teach music to produce prodigies. Instead, we teach music to open up their world, to give them tools for learning, self-expression, and connection.*

Sadly, I've met many parents who stopped music lessons because their child "didn't like it" or "didn't have natural talent."

This breaks my heart because it misses the point. We'd never stop teaching a child to speak just because they don't enjoy practicing words. Music, like language, is a fundamental skill that enriches life, whether your child becomes a musician or not.

The House Where Five Kids Compose (and Nobody's a Prodigy)

I still smile every time I think about the message I got from a homeschooling mom in the Pacific Northwest who has five children under nine.

Mom plays piano; Dad grew up singing in a church choir. Music isn't an "extra" in their house; it's oxygen. They sing together, dance to Vivaldi, and end every night with lullabies.

But the moment that stopped me in my tracks was this: Their eight and seven-year-old daughters started composing their own little songs, nothing fancy, just melodies they loved and then wrote the notes down so their four-year-old and two-year-old sisters could play them too.

No one told them composing was "advanced." No one told them they had to wait for a teacher's permission. They just heard music all day, every day, in a house that treated it like breathing. The four-year-old practiced "Joy to the World" for a month, on her own, while Mom folded laundry nearby.

That's what happens when music isn't a subject. It becomes a family language everyone gets to speak, even the baby. Your home can sound like that too. Five kids, one piano, zero prodigies required.

Just love, repetition, and a lot of shared melodies.

■ Try This at Home

Sing and Move Game

Pick a favorite nursery rhyme like "Itsy Bitsy Spider." Sing it with your child, adding hand motions to match the words (e.g., fingers crawling for the spider). Then, let your child invent new motions or silly sounds. This builds rhythm, coordination, and creativity while making music a joyful, shared experience.

■ Parent Takeaway

You don't need to be a musician to teach your child music, just like you don't need to be a chef to cook with them. Every song you sing or rhythm you clap is building your child's brain and heart, skills that will help them in school, friendships, and beyond.

Why Music Affects the Brain So Deeply

Growing up bilingual in Spanish and English, I've always been amazed by how naturally language flows through me. I don't remember learning Spanish, it's just part of who I am.

But here's what's even more incredible: learning Spanish didn't just teach me a language; it gave me a growth mindset. To this day, I approach new challenges, whether it's mastering a new instrument or tackling a complex project, with the confidence that I can learn anything.

> *"I'm convinced those early years of absorbing language set the stage for a lifetime of curiosity and resilience."*

Music has a similar power. In the first few years of life, a child's brain is a whirlwind of neural activity, forming connections at an astonishing rate. When you sing a lullaby or clap a rhythm with your child, you're not just teaching music, you're shaping how their brain learns.

Research shows that activities like music engage multiple brain regions at once. The *temporal lobe* processes sounds, the *motor cortex* coordinates movement, the *frontal lobe* handles focus, and the l*imbic system* ties it all to emotion. This is why music feels so natural and joyful, it's a full-brain workout! Compare this to reading, another brain-intensive activity.

> *A 2020 Harvard study explains that reading involves the temporal lobe (for decoding sounds), Broca's area (for language comprehension), and the angular gyrus (for connecting letters to words) (Dehaene et al., 2020, p. 429).*

Music goes even further, engaging these areas plus motor and emotional regions. For example, when your child sings

"Twinkle, Twinkle, Little Star" while clapping the beat, they're strengthening auditory processing, fine motor skills, memory, and emotional connection, all at once. This is why music is such a powerful tool for early development.

■ Did You Know?

Music Builds Grit
Music activities improve self-regulation and problem-solving in children (Williams et al., 2018). Resilience in every note!

Active vs. Passive Music: Why Participation Matters

Let's talk about the difference between *hearing* music and *making* music. Think about a time you told a story to someone who was only half-listening, maybe nodding along while scrolling on their phone. They heard your words, but they didn't truly process them. That's *passive listening*.

Now, imagine telling the same story to someone who's fully engaged, asking questions and reacting. That's *active listening*, and it's a completely different experience.

Music works the same way. Passive music exposure, like hearing a song on the radio or a movie soundtrack, has some benefits, like setting a mood or sparking memories. But it's active participation that transforms a child's brain.

Active Music = Full-Brain Workout.

Clap rhythm → Focus ← Passive: Radio song

Motor Cortex (Movement) ← Active: Clapping game

Limbic System (Emotion) ← Active: Singing with you

When your child sings, claps, or dances to music, they're lighting up neural pathways for focus, memory, and coordination. For example, a simple game of clapping a rhythm back and forth with your child builds auditory processing (temporal lobe), movement control (motor cortex), and turn-taking (social-emotional circuits). Unlike endless drills, music is inherently fun, so kids dive in without resistance.

This is an important philosophy of learning at Color Me Mozart. It's designed to make active music participation easy and joyful for parents and kids.

For instance, try turning a car ride into a music adventure by singing a song and tapping the steering wheel to the beat, then inviting your child to join in. These moments don't just teach music, they build skills that help your child in school, friendships, and life.

■ Try This at Home

Kitchen Band Jam
Grab some kitchen items (spoons, pots, plastic containers) and turn them into instruments. Tap a simple rhythm on a pot, then let your child copy or create their own. Add a favorite song and take turns leading the "band." This boosts rhythm, creativity, and listening skills.

■ Parent Takeaway

Active music-making is like a gym for your child's brain. Every time you sing, clap, or dance together, you're helping them develop focus, coordination, and empathy, skills that will make them stronger learners and kinder friends.

Bringing Music Back Home

Somewhere along the way, we started treating music education like an elite skill, reserved for the "talented" or those destined to perform. A century ago, families sang together, played instruments, and passed down songs like cherished heirlooms.

Today, we often outsource music to specialists, leaving parents feeling unqualified. But just as you teach your child to count or tie their shoes, you can teach them music. You don't need to be a professional, just a parent who's willing to have fun and make memories.

The real purpose of early music education is to enrich your child's life, not to create a prodigy. It's about giving them tools to think, feel, and connect in ways that will serve them forever. When you sing a silly song during bath time or clap a rhythm while waiting at the doctor's office, you're not just passing the time, you're wiring your child's brain for learning and building a bond that lasts a lifetime.

So, let's rethink music education. It's not about perfection or performance, it's about play, connection, and growth. You've already got everything you need to be your child's first music teacher. Let's make music a part of your family's story.

By embracing music as a tool for growth, you're giving your child a gift that goes far beyond the melodies. So, grab a spoon, sing a song, and start this joyful journey together. You've got this!

■ Did You Know?

Music Strengthens Bonds

Group music activities enhance social cohesion and cooperation in children (Kirschner & Ilari, 2021). Singing together builds family ties!

■ Chapter Recap

1. **Music Is More Than Notes**: Like sports, music teaches life skills—focus, resilience, empathy—that shape your child beyond the activity itself.
2. **It's Not About Talent**: Early music education isn't about creating prodigies; it's about enriching your child's brain, body, and heart.
3. **Active Participation Is Key**: Singing, clapping, or dancing engages more of your child's brain than passive listening, boosting learning and development.
4. **You're the Perfect Teacher**: Just as you teach your child to speak or count, you can teach them music with simple, fun activities with no prior training needed.

Chapter 4

What Gets in the Way

> *We are the music makers, and we are the dreamers of dreams.*
>
> —Arthur William Edgar O'Shaughnessy

When I was in junior high, I somehow found myself on the track and field team, which was a bit of a surprise since running wasn't exactly my thing. My world revolved around soccer, skateboarding, and video games, not exactly a résumé for a track star.

I think perhaps the coach saw me sprinting across the schoolyard one day and figured I'd be a decent fit. I wasn't so sure. I doubted I had what it took to compete, but no one told me, "You're not a runner!" or laughed me off the team. So, I gave it a shot, thinking, "What's the worst that can happen?"

Spoiler alert: I didn't win any gold medals or find myself on any highlight reels. My track "career" was short, literally one meet, to be exact, but I held my own, especially for someone with zero training. Looking back, I'm grateful no one discouraged me.

That experience left me with fun memories and a valuable lesson that stayed with me: trying something new, even if you're not "gifted," can open doors you never expected. It's a lesson I carried into my music journey, which began years later on the fateful day in high school when I chose to take the music class.

That's a spirit we strive to embrace at Color Me Mozart. Even if you doubt your "musical" abilities, you can overcome the barriers and make music a joyful part of your family's story.

■ Did You Know?

Rhythm Is Wired into You

Even seven-month-olds detect rhythmic patterns in language and music (Hannon et al., 2019). Rhythm is instinct—no degree needed!

"I'm Not Musical": Where That Belief Comes From

Have you ever said, "I'm not musical" or "I have no rhythm"? I hear this all the time from parents, and it breaks my heart because it's rarely true. Let's go back to my track story. I wasn't a natural runner, but no one told me I couldn't do it, so I tried. Imagine if someone had said, "You're not athletic, stick to video games." I might have believed them and missed out on a great experience.

Too often, the belief that we're "not musical" comes from a single moment, a teacher's harsh comment, a failed piano lesson, or a friend laughing at our off-key singing. Those moments stick with us, shaping how we see ourselves.

In my case, music wasn't a big part of my childhood. We had a piano in our Brooklyn apartment, but it was more a shelf for knick-knacks than an instrument. As I mentioned, it was only in high school when I first truly heard it played. Having had no prior musical experience, when I started music class, I was probably the least likely candidate to become a musician.

Yet, that class with Mr. Rubin (you might remember him trolling us with "The Star-Spangled Banner") showed me music was accessible to all of us, not just for the "gifted." I meet parents who say they're "tone-deaf" or "have two left feet" for rhythm, often because of one bad experience, maybe a choir teacher who told them to "just mouth the words" or a piano lesson that felt impossible.

Here's the truth: children don't start out believing they're "bad" at anything. They're naturally curious, eager to try new things, like when your toddler bangs on pots or sings made-up songs. As I often say, *"Children naturally believe they can until they're told they can't."*

To prove you *are* musical, let's try a fun activity together. Read the opening of the famous Christmas poem by Clement Clarke Moore aloud:

> *'Twas the night before Christmas,*
> *when all through the house,*
> *Not a creature was stirring,*
> *not even a mouse.*

Chances are, you read it with a natural rhythm, emphasizing *"Twas the NIGHT be-fore CHRISTmas."* That's literary rhythm is called anapestic tetrameter, but don't worry about the fancy term, the important thing is that you instinctively read it with the correct intonations. This simple example proves that you indeed do have rhythm, just like you have the instinct to teach your child language.

The belief that you're "not musical" is not innate, it's learned, often from a discouraging moment. The good news? You can unlearn it and help your child avoid those doubts altogether.

■ Try This at Home

Rhythm Echo Game

Clap a simple pattern (e.g., clap-clap-pause-clap) and have your child echo it back. Then let them create a pattern for you to copy. Add fun twists like tapping on a table or using silly voices. This builds rhythm and confidence while showing music is playful, not perfect.

■ Parent Takeaway

You're more musical than you think. Just like you naturally read a poem with rhythm, you can teach your child music with simple games and songs—no expertise needed.

Overcoming the Intimidation of Instruments and Music Theory

When I walked into my high school music class, the piano felt like a spaceship, 88 keys, all black or white, staring back at me. Growing up, that piano in our apartment was silent, a piece of furniture my parents rarely touched. I had no clue how anyone could turn those keys into music.

But when Mr. Rubin played, I was hooked. I wanted to figure it out, just like I loved puzzling over how things worked as a kid, thanks to my dad's endless questions about the world, why the sky is blue, how bridges stand. That curiosity drove me to see the piano not as intimidating, but as a puzzle to solve.

Many parents feel overwhelmed by instruments or music theory, thinking they need to master sheet music or play like a pro to teach their kids. I get it, those funny-looking symbols (notes, rests, clefs) can seem like a foreign code. But here's the secret: music is just another language, like the Spanish I learned from my parents.

It has an alphabet (A–G, just seven letters compared to English's 26), patterns, and rules that anyone can learn step by

Music is simpler than you think.

ENGLISH ALPHABET	♫ MUSICAL ALPHABET
26 Letters: A to Z	7 Notes: A B C D E F G
Full sentences → Years to master	Simple songs → Weeks to sing

step. You don't need to be fluent from day one, just like you didn't expect your child to speak full sentences as a toddler.

Think about how you taught your child to talk. You started with simple words like "mama" or "cat" and built from there. Music works the same way. You don't need to teach your child to read sheet music right away. Instead, start with clapping rhythms or singing nursery rhymes. Instruments? They're not as scary as they look.

A piano's keys follow repeatable patterns. In fact, I'll teach you how to identify each key on the piano in a later chapter. Even simple instruments like a tambourine or xylophone are intuitive for kids. At Color Me Mozart, we've broken music down into bite-sized pieces, so you and your child can explore together without feeling overwhelmed. It's like learning the ABCs, one step at a time, leading to fluency.

■ Did You Know?

Music Boosts Confidence

Informal music activities build self-esteem and confidence in trying new tasks (Hallam, 2020). Music lets kids succeed in a low-pressure way.

■ Try This at Home

Sing-Along Story

Pick a favorite storybook and make up a simple song about the characters or plot (e.g., “The bear went over the mountain”). Sing it with your child, adding claps or stomps to the beat. This connects music to storytelling, making it fun and familiar.

■ Parent Takeaway

Instruments and music theory are just tools, like letters in the alphabet. Start small with songs and rhythms, and you’ll see music isn’t as complex as it seems.

Creating a Guilt-Free, Judgment-Free Space at Home

Last summer, I led a music camp at our church for young kids, and on the first day, I asked, "Who likes to fail?" The kids looked at me like I was nuts and to no ones surprise, no hands went up. I get it. Failure sounds like a bad word. But here's the thing: failure is how we learn. Throughout the week, we changed our thinking and redefined the concept of failing or making mistakes. *"The faster you fail, the faster you succeed,"* we chanted, turning it into a catchy slogan.

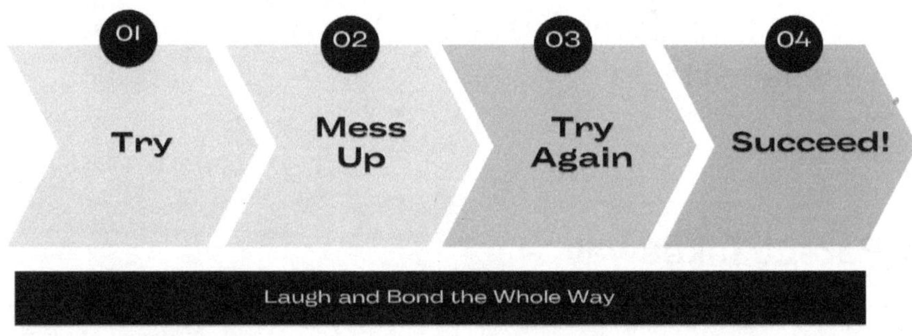

By the end of the camp, the kids were in a different state of mind as they tried new songs and rhythms, unafraid to mess up. That's the kind of environment I want you to create at home of your family with music.

When I started piano in high school, I made plenty of mistakes, playing wrong notes and having clumsy fingers. But Mr. Rubin never made me feel "bad" for trying. In fact, he celebrated every attempt, just like my parents cheered my first Spanish words, even when they were far from perfect.

Too often, parents worry about "pushing" their kids or fear they'll fail because they're not "musical" themselves. But music isn't about perfection, it's about play. When you create a judgment-free space, your child can experiment, make mistakes, and grow confident.

Imagine if your child was struggling to read a certain word. You wouldn't say, "You're not a gifted reader, you should just quit!" Quite the opposite, you'd encourage them to sound it out, try again, and celebrate their effort. Music deserves the same approach. You can and should make music a natural part of your day, singing during bath time, tapping rhythms at dinner. These moments aren't about getting it "right"; they're about joy and connection.

When your child feels safe to try, fail, and try again, music becomes a language they *live*, not a skill they're judged on.

■ Did You Know?

Mistakes Accelerate Learning

Kids in mistake-friendly settings master skills 40% faster (Moser et al., 2017). Safe failure = super learning!

■ Try This at Home

Music Scavenger Hunt

Hunt five household "instruments." Make a 30-second song. Record it on your phone. Play back and cheer every squeak.

Bringing It All Together

The barriers to teaching music, feeling "unmusical," fearing instruments, or worrying about failure are real, but they're not insurmountable. Just as I overcame my doubts on the track field and at the piano, you can overcome yours.

You don't need to be a musician to teach your child music, just like you don't need to be a linguist to teach them to talk. With simple activities, a playful spirit, and a safe space, you can make music a vibrant part of your family's life. Think back to my bilingual home. Learning Spanish from my parents wasn't about perfection, it was about connection, repetition, and joy. And it is a joy that I carry with me to this day.

Learning music is the same. Every clap, every song, every silly dance is a step toward fluency, wiring your child's brain for learning and building memories you'll both cherish.

At Color Me Mozart, we've made it easy to break through these barriers, so you can start today, no matter your background. You're not just teaching music, you're opening a world of possibility for your child.

■ Parent Takeaway

Mistakes are the stepping stones to music fluency. Create a home where your child feels free to experiment, and you'll both discover the joy of learning together.

■ Chapter Recap

1. **You Are Musical**: The belief that you're "not musical" often comes from a single negative experience, not a lack of ability. Rhythm and music are already part of you, just like language.
2. **Instruments Aren't Scary**: Music theory and instruments are learnable, like the alphabet. Start with simple songs and rhythms, and build from there.
3. **Failure Is Your Friend**: Mistakes are essential for learning. A judgment-free home lets your child explore music with confidence.
4. **Color Me Mozart Breaks Barriers**: With parent-friendly activities, you can make music a natural, joyful part of your day, no expertise required.
5. **Focus on Fluency, Not Perfection**: Like teaching your child to talk, music is about connection and growth, not prodigy-level skill.

Part III

Music As a Language: And You're Already Speaking It

Chapter 5

Sound Is The First Instrument

> *Where words leave off, music begins.*
>
> —Heinrich Heine

When I think about how I learned Spanish as a child, I'm amazed at how effortlessly it became a part of me. Growing up, our Brooklyn apartment was filled with the sounds of Spanish words, intonations, and rhythms that shaped my bilingual world. But music? That was quieter.

We had a piano, but it sat silent, more a piece of furniture than an instrument, as I discovered in high school when that first music class changed my life. That silence piano didn't stop me from absorbing sound, though. The hum of cartoons, the jingles on TV, even the cadence of my parents' speech, they were all planting seeds for the musician I'd become. Sound, I've learned, is our first instrument, and it's where your child's music journey begins too. At Color Me Mozart, we believe you can turn everyday sounds into a joyful path to music fluency, with no expertise required.

Think about how your child learned to talk. By age five, they're using thousands of words, 2,000 to 2,500, according to research, picking up 10–20 new ones each week between ages two and six.

That's incredible!

They don't learn this from flashcards or formal lessons; they learn by listening, imitating, and playing with sounds.

Coos turn into "mama," words become phrases, and soon they're telling you stories about their day. This natural process, from hearing to speaking, is how children learn any language, including music.

Listening → Imitating → Speaking.

Same for music.

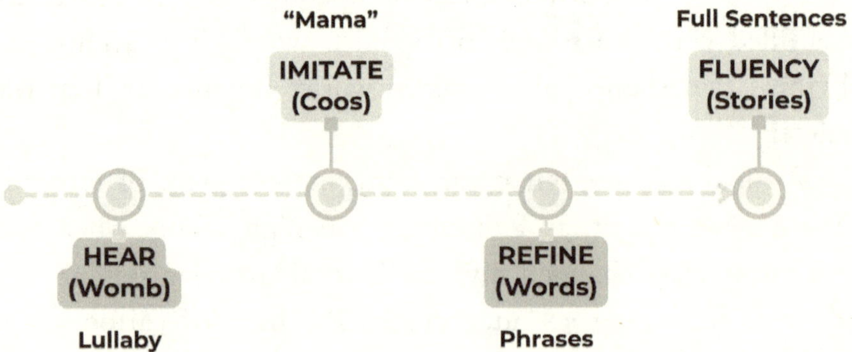

As their first teacher, you can create a sound-rich environment that sets the stage for music fluency, just as you did for language.

■ Did You Know?

Your Baby's First Concert Hall
Newborns prefer lullabies heard in utero (Partanen et al., 2013). Your heartbeat and hums are their first playlist.

Children Learn Music "By Ear"

Musicians often talk about playing "by ear." That simply means being able to hear a melody and then recreate it on an instrument with no sheet music required.

When we play by ear, the brain builds a *direct connection between sound and motion*. It skips the visual step entirely. We hear something, then our hands (or voice) reproduce it.

This is exactly what children do with language. Long before they can read, they're practicing sound-to-motor mapping. They hear, they imitate, and they refine until words form naturally.

No one would dream of handing a newborn a book and saying, "Start reading!" We know instinctively that listening must come first. The same principle applies to music. Before reading notes, children must *hear* and *feel* them.

That's why your role as a parent-teacher is so powerful. You can create a rich sound environment that is full of music, rhythm, and joyful imitation, just as you did with language.

The House Where Music Is the Heartbeat

Ksenia lives on a small farm with her husband, her three children, chickens, cats, and skies that go on forever. She's an artist and photographer and her husband keeps the rhythm of the land.

And in their home, music isn't scheduled, it just breathes. Mornings might begin with the boys at the piano while their sister stretches for ballet. The afternoon might find someone humming an old Russian lullaby Ksenia's mother sang to her decades ago, now drifting through the kitchen while bread rises and the cat naps on the windowsill.

Given her Russian heritage, Ksenia understands the importance of starting early with learning multiple languages. That is why she has made it a point to teach her children to speak not only Russian and English, but has also added French to their routine.

In addition to the multiple spoken and written languages already mentioned, she has also included art and music as part of their curriculum. Ksenia and her husband value the ruches that only music and art can bring into the lives of a child.

That is why music is ever present in their home. Music is the background track to feeding animals, sketching wildflowers, chasing golden-hour photos across the fields, and editing pictures late into the evening. Ksenia wrote, "I don't separate music, art, homeschooling, or country living. They're all expressions of the same thing: being present."

That's the secret so many families discover once they let music move in. It stops being something you "do" for thirty minutes. It becomes the heartbeat of the home. And the children grow up fluent, without ever noticing they were learning. Your house can sound like that too. All it takes is letting the music play while life happens around it.

■ Try This at Home

Sound Safari

Grab a laundry basket. Hunt five household "instruments" (keys, spoon, cereal box). Play each one, name its sound ("jingly," "thumpy"), then mix them into a 20-second family band. Record it. Play it back at dinner. Instant hit single.

■ Parent Takeaway

Your child learns music the same way they learn to talk. by listening and imitating. Fill their world with sounds, and they'll start "speaking" music naturally.

How Fluency Begins with Hearing and Movement

What does "music fluency" mean? It's not about playing a concerto or singing perfectly, it's about ease and comfort with music, just like speaking a language. Merriam-Webster defines fluency as "the ability to use a language easily and accurately" or "mastery of a subject." For your child, music fluency means clapping a rhythm, singing a tune, or dancing to a beat with confidence and joy. And it all starts with sound and movement.

Babies are born ready to absorb sound. From the third trimester, they're tuning into rhythms and melodies, as Susan Rogers pointed out in *This Is What It Sounds Like*.

In his book *Musicophilia,* Oliver Sacks points out that the rhythms that babies hear in their first year, such as those found in lullabies, nursery rhymes, even the beat of footsteps, become their "home base" rhythms for life. In other words, those are the rhythms they will feel most comfortable with for the rest of their lives (Sacks, 2007, p. 246).

Growing up, I heard fairly simple rhythms in TV jingles, nursery rhymes, and songs on the radio. These songs typically had straightforward rhythms that were easy to count along with. I could nod my head and count 1-2-3-4 with no problem at all.

More complex rhythms, however, like those found in jazz or salsa, were more challenging for me because they weren't part of my early soundscape. They emphasized off-beats or "in-between" pulses, which musicians call *syncopation*, and my brain had to work harder to feel them.

For me, simple rhythms felt like this:

> *Listen ➡ Feel ➡ Play ➡ Dance.*

Complex one were more like this:

> *Listen ➡ Kinda Feel ➡ Play with Effort ➡ Not Dance (at least, not without looking awkward!)*

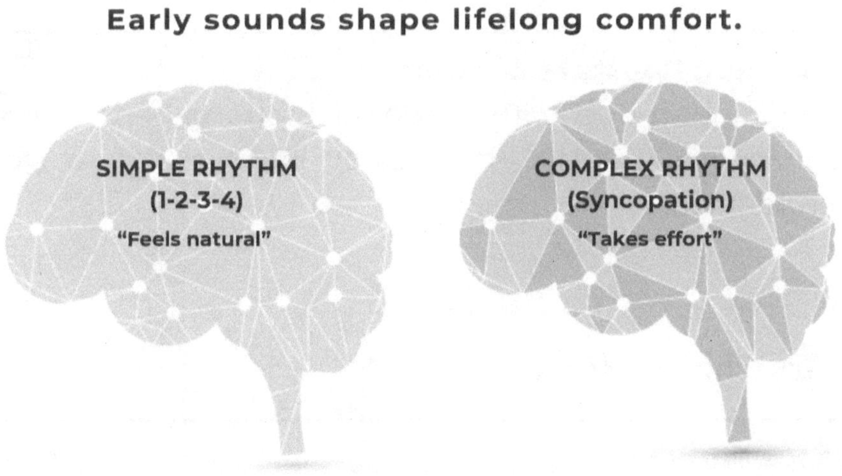

Early sounds shape lifelong comfort.

Your child's brain works the same way, soaking up the sounds you surround them with. That is why I always encourage parents to play many different styles and genres of music for their kids. More on that later.

When you add movement to music, it makes those rhythms stick even more. For instance, when you sing a song such as "Itsy

Bitsy Spider" and wiggle your fingers, your child isn't just having fun, they're wiring their brain to connect sound to motion. This builds skills like coordination, listening accuracy, and emotional expression. In my preschool classes, students would light up when we clapped along to a song like "If You're Happy and You Know It." In the end, they weren't just learning rhythm and movement; they were learning teamwork, creativity, and self-awareness, all through play.

■ Did You Know?

Movement Boosts Music Learning
Combining music with movement strengthens neural connections (Gordon et al., 2019). Every clap is a step toward fluency.

■ Try This at Home

Dance Party Freeze
Play a favorite song and dance with your child. When you pause the music, everyone freezes. Take turns choosing actions (e.g., spin, jump). This teaches rhythm, listening, and body control while keeping it silly and fun.

■ Parent Takeaway

Pairing music with movement—like dancing or clapping—makes learning stick. It's not just play; it's building your child's brain and body for music and beyond.

Sound Recognition and Active Listening

Active listening is like a superpower for kids. Imagine you're at a park, and amid the chatter, a bird chirps loudly. Your child turns, noticing the sound. That's their brain at work, picking out patterns and differences in pitch, tone, or rhythm. This skill doesn't just happen, it's built through exposure and attention. When you point out sounds—a guitar in a song, the hum of a fridge, or rain on the window—you're helping your child create neural pathways for listening precision.

In my high school music class, I learned to pick out the piano's notes amid Mr. Rubin's playing. It was like solving a puzzle, and it made music feel alive. You can do the same for your child. Play a song in the car and ask, "Do you hear the drums? The singer's voice?" Over time, they'll spot sounds faster than you can. This isn't just about music—it boosts language and reading skills too, as the same brain areas handle both. With Color Me Mozart, you can turn everyday moments into listening games, making sound the foundation of your child's music journey.

Bringing Sound to Life

Sound is everywhere, and it's your child's first instrument. Before they sing, play, or read notes, they listen. That's where music fluency begins, just like language. You don't need to be a musician to guide this process, just a parent who fills your home with sound. Sing during bath time, tap rhythms at dinner, or dance in the living room. These moments aren't just fun; they're shaping your child's brain, building skills like focus, coordination, and emotional connection.

With Color Me Mozart, I've made it easy to weave sound into your day. You don't need a piano or sheet music, just your voice, a few household items, and a willingness to play. Every hum, clap, or silly song is a note in your child's musical story, one that you're writing together. So, turn up the sounds in your home, and watch your child become fluent in the language of music.

■ Did You Know?

Sound Recognition Builds Reading Skills
Identifying musical/environmental sounds boosts phonological awareness (Kraus & White-Schwoch, 2021). Listening helps reading!

■ Parent Takeaway

Every sound your child notices, whether a bird or a beat, builds their "sound vocabulary." Make listening a game, and you're setting them up for music and language fluency.

■ Try This at Home

Sound Story Time
Read a favorite book and add sound effects for actions (e.g., clap for footsteps, hum for wind). Let your child add their own sounds. This connects listening to storytelling, sparking creativity and musical awareness.

■ Chapter Recap

1. **Sound Is the Foundation**: Babies start hearing music and rhythms in the womb, setting the stage for fluency in both language and music.
2. **Learn By Ear First**: Just like speaking, music begins with listening and imitating, not reading notes, making it accessible for every parent and child.
3. **Movement Amplifies Learning**: Clapping, dancing, or singing with actions strengthens your child's musical and motor skills, all through play.
4. **Early Sounds Shape Lifelong Patterns**: The rhythms your child hears in their first year become their musical "home base," so surround them with variety.
5. **Active Listening Builds Skills**: Noticing sounds in music or the environment sharpens focus and boosts language and reading readiness.

Chapter 6

Singing, Speaking, and Musical Imitation

> *Music is the universal language of mankind.*
>
> —Henry Wadsworth Longfellow

I remember the first time I bought a book in Spanish. I was visiting family in Buenos Aires, wandering through one of those old neighborhood bookstores that smell like paper and history. I wasn't looking for anything specific, just browsing, as book lovers do. There's something magical about running your fingers along the spines, cracking open a new one, and feeling that satisfying texture of a fresh page.

Somewhere between the shelves, I had a sudden realization: How did I even know how to read Spanish? My parents never sat me down for "Spanish lessons." We didn't have grammar workbooks or vocabulary charts at home. Yet there I was, flipping through novels and understanding everything.

That moment stuck with me. If no one ever formally taught me to read Spanish, when and how did I learn? The answer, as I would later come to understand, lies in the way the brain builds and transfers neural maps. Because I had heard and spoken Spanish from a young age, my brain already had a road map for the language.

When reading came along, it simply borrowed the structure I had already developed for English and applied it effortlessly to Spanish. I'm aware that many people never get to experience this phenomenon because they grow up speaking one language.

In many countries in Europe, however, growing up with two languages is the norm. Perhaps you've had the chance to visit a European city and may have been surprised to see so many people able to speak English quite well. That wasn't the result of an app on their phone, that was an intentional effort put forth by their parents and their culture.

And I'm not unique in this. My sisters had the same experience, as have countless children growing up in bilingual homes. Their brains didn't wait for formal instruction; they learned through exposure, repetition, and imitation. This same principle is the foundation of musical fluency.

Just as a child doesn't wait for school to learn to talk, they shouldn't wait for music lessons to start learning the language of music. The earlier a child hears and imitates, the deeper the neural connections become.

Think about how we acquire language: we listen before we ever speak. Babies don't come with grammar textbooks; they come with the innate ability to absorb sound. From the first moments of life and even before birth, children are mapping tone, rhythm, and emotional inflection. That's why the steady stream of spoken language from parents, siblings, and caregivers is so essential in the early years.

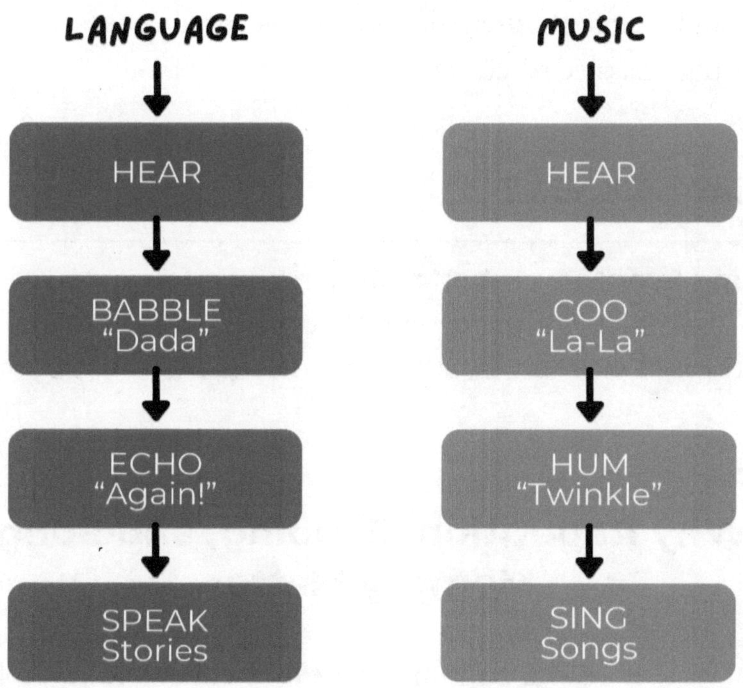

Imagine if we waited until kindergarten to start speaking to our children. Their language development would be delayed, no matter how intelligent or capable they are. The same is true for music.

We can't rely solely on background noise, cartoon songs, car radio tunes, or music playing faintly in stores. Those are passive listening experiences. They're fine as a starting point, but they don't build true fluency. Fluency requires active participation. Singing together, imitating sounds, and moving to rhythm, that's where the magic happens.

When children are encouraged to respond to music, they're not just hearing; they're processing, decoding, and expressing. This kind of musical conversation strengthens both sides of the brain and helps children become active participants in sound rather than passive receivers.

■ Did You Know?

Singing Syncs Parent and Child
Parent-infant singing synchronizes heartbeats and breathing (Feldman, 2020). Your voice is their first bond.

Why Repetition, Echoing, and Song Memory Matter

If you've ever read a bedtime story to a child, you've probably been through this routine: you close the book, ready to turn off the light, and they say, "Again!" You read it again. And again. And again, until you can recite the story by heart. That insistent repetition isn't stubbornness. It's how the brain learns best.

When a child hears or sings the same song repeatedly, the brain is carving and reinforcing neural pathways. It's like walking the same forest trail every day. At first the path is overgrown, but each step clears it a little more until it becomes smooth and familiar. That's fluency being built in real time.

The same process happens when children hear and echo back sounds. In music, this is known as call and response, one person sings or plays a short phrase, and the other imitates it.

In language, it's exactly what happens when a baby babbles and a parent responds. This back-and-forth communication builds the bridge between hearing and doing, between sound and expression.

Every repetition strengthens the connection. That's why familiar songs are such powerful tools. The first time a child hears a melody, they're absorbing pitch and rhythm. The second time, they might hum along. The third time, they anticipate what comes next. And before long, they're not only singing the melody but doing so confidently, with timing and phrasing that match the original.

Repetition also builds muscle memory, coordination, and emotional connection. When a child sings a song with joy or comfort, especially when it's shared with a parent, their brain pairs that emotional experience with the sound itself. That's why songs from childhood stay with us for decades.

Even adults experience this phenomenon. Have you ever remembered every lyric to a song you haven't heard in twenty years? That's not nostalgia alone, it's your brain's dedicated music memory network at work.

Unlike many other memories, musical ones are stored in multiple regions of the brain, which is why people with Alzheimer's can often recall and sing songs long after other memories fade. So when your child asks for the same song again and again, remember: their brain isn't just seeking entertainment, it's building the foundation for lifelong musical fluency.

And as an added bonus, repetition teaches patience, focus, and collaboration. In call-and-response singing, children practice waiting their turn, listening carefully, and celebrating others' participation. In the process, they're not only learning music; they're learning empathy, timing, and teamwork.

In my preschool classes, I saw this when kids sang "Wheels on the Bus" over and over, taking turns leading verses. They weren't just singing, they were learning to connect.

■ Try This at Home

Call-and-Response Sing-Along

Sing a simple phrase like "La, la, la" in a fun melody, and have your child echo it back. Change the pitch or speed each time, letting them mimic you. Add silly words or sounds to keep it playful. This builds listening, imitation, and confidence.

■ Parent Takeaway

Repetition is your child's secret weapon for learning music. Every time they sing or echo a song, they're building fluency, just like they did with words.

Ear-First Learning Activities (Just Like How We Learn to Talk)

Think back to how you first learned to speak. Before you ever formed words, you listened. You heard voices rising and falling, sentences repeating, rhythms of speech filling the air around you. No one handed you a rulebook or a grammar chart, you absorbed language by ear.

The same process builds musical understanding. Long before a child can read music or understand what a "C major scale" is, they're listening, noticing patterns, and trying to imitate. Babies hear tone and rhythm and slowly begin to echo them back, first as coos and babbles, then as short melodies and words.

In everyday life, this imitation is happening constantly. When a baby laughs because you laughed, or claps because you clapped, that's musical imitation in its earliest form. Those tiny responses are laying the groundwork for coordination, timing, and communication.

Scientists call this *auditory-motor mapping*: the process by which the brain links what it hears with how the body responds. Each time your child hears a sound and reproduces it, whether by singing, tapping, or humming, the connection between hearing and movement strengthens. These neural bridges are the very same ones used for speech, rhythm, and reading later in life.

That's why the first phase of learning, what I call ear-first learning, is so powerful. During this stage, the goal isn't perfection but participation. The more your child listens, imitates, and experiments, the faster their fluency grows.

Imagine, for example, a simple game of echoing short phrases. You sing, "La, la, la," and your child sings it back. You vary the notes or tempo; they try again. To them, it feels like play. To their brain, it's deep training in pitch recognition, rhythm, and memory.

Even more important is that these activities are relational. A child learns best when sound is tied to emotion and connection. The joy of sharing a song with you, the laughter, the eye contact, the physical movement—creates a web of positive associations around music. That's what keeps them coming back to it again and again.

Music and movement songs like *The Hokey Pokey* or *If You're Happy and You Know It* are perfect examples. While they seem simple, they engage nearly every part of the brain. To "put your left hand in and take your left hand out" requires timing, body awareness, coordination, and listening, all synchronized to rhythm and words. Every repetition strengthens the brain's sense of pattern, timing, and balance.

Over time, your child begins to connect musical feeling with expression. The gentle sway of a lullaby signals calm; a lively rhythm sparks energy. This emotional vocabulary is what allows music to become a language of its own. And here's the good news: none of this requires formal lessons or special talent. You don't need to play an instrument to start. Simply make music an active part of your daily rhythm, sing during cleanup, echo sounds in the car, hum before bed. Each of these moments is a building block toward musical fluency.

■ Did You Know?

Singing Boosts Language Skills
Singing enhances vocabulary and phonological awareness (Williams et al., 2018). Your lullabies teach reading!

■ Try This at Home

Mirror Song Game
Sing a short phrase from a favorite song (e.g., "Twinkle, twinkle, little star") and have your child mirror it back. Take turns leading, adding claps or funny voices. This builds imitation, rhythm, and emotional connection.

■ Parent Takeaway

Your voice is your child's best music teacher. Singing together, even if you're not "perfect," builds fluency and bonds you through shared joy.

Expanding the Sound World

Many parents stop at the "music-and-movement" stage, thinking that more advanced learning demands a teacher or an instrument. But children thrive on variety. Once they're comfortable singing and moving, introduce new sounds and styles.

Let them hear classical pieces, Latin rhythms, jazz, bluegrass, anything that broadens their ear. Exposure builds flexibility. The more kinds of music they hear, the more rhythmic and melodic patterns their brain can recognize and reproduce. This diversity will later make it easier for them to read notation, keep time, and improvise.

You can turn this into an adventure. Pick a day of the week to explore a new genre. Listen to a Mozart symphony while drawing, a Tito Puente salsa while cooking, or a Miles Davis tune during breakfast. Ask questions: How does this make you feel? What instruments do you hear? These small conversations teach children that music isn't a subject, it's an experience.

■ Did You Know?

Music Strengthens Empathy
Group singing builds empathy and cooperation (Gerry et al., 2016). Shared songs wire hearts.

■ Try This at Home

Genre Journey Night

Pick a new music style each week (e.g., jazz, folk, classical). Play a song during dinner and ask your child, "What do you hear? How does it feel?" Dance or clap along. This expands their musical world and sparks curiosity.

■ Parent Takeaway

Variety in music is like variety in food—it nourishes your child's brain. Explore new sounds together, and you're building a richer musical vocabulary.

Bringing It All Together

When you combine listening, imitation, movement, and emotion, you give your child everything they need to become fluent in the language of music. You're not just training their ear; you're shaping attention, empathy, and memory. Each repeated song, each echoed phrase, each shared laugh while singing together, these are the invisible lessons that make music a lifelong companion rather than a school subject.

And perhaps the most beautiful part: you're already equipped to do this. Every parent, regardless of musical background, can sing, hum, or move to music. What matters most is presence, your willingness to share sound intentionally with your child. That's how fluency begins: one sound, one echo, one joyful imitation at a time.

■ Did You Know?

Music Memories Last a Lifetime

Musical memories resist Alzheimer's due to multi-region storage (Jacobsen et al., 2017). Songs today = memories forever.

■ Parent Reflection

What songs filled your own childhood? Which melodies still surface in your mind without effort? Now imagine your child twenty years from today. What songs will bring them back to these early moments with you? Start singing those songs now. They'll remember them forever.

■ Chapter Recap

1. **Exposure Creates Fluency**: Children learn music through listening and imitation, just like language, without needing formal lessons.
2. **Repetition Builds Pathways**: Each repeated song strengthens neural connections, fostering confidence and musical memory.
3. **Ear-First Learning Is Natural**: Singing and imitating sounds come before reading notes, mirroring how children learn to speak.
4. **Emotion Locks in Learning**: Songs shared with love and joy create lasting memories and emotional bonds.
5. **Variety Expands Understanding**: Exposing kids to different genres builds a flexible musical vocabulary, making future learning easier.
6. **Parents Are the First Teachers**: Your voice and enthusiasm are all your child needs to start their musical journey with Color Me Mozart.

Chapter 7

Rhythm and Routine as Your Curriculum

> *Music . . . can name the unnameable and communicate the unknowable.*
>
> —Leonard Bernstein

If I asked you to describe the concept of *rhythm* to me, you may have a hard time putting it into words. As hard as it would be to describe in words, you can certainly feel rhythm intrinsically. To explain rhythm, you may even resort to clapping, dancing a bit, or perhaps even doing a simple beatbox demo.

When I began learning music, I also would have had a har time describing exactly what rhythm meant but I sure felt it in my bones. One of the first bands I ever got to see live was Rush. In case you are not familiar with them, they are a Canadian progressive rock trio that were known for their virtuosity and musicianship. The funny thing was I was not a Rush fan but my buddy George, who is a drummer, was what we would call a super fan. He would see them live all the time and talk about them like they were the greatest band of all time. During one of their tours, George invited me to go with him to see them live. I loved seeing live music in general so I was more than happy to go with him.

As soon as the house lights went dim and the stage lit up, and the concert started, I knew this band was something special. No background music, just three musicians on stage creating a huge amount of music. I couldn't figure out where all that music was coming from. How could three musicians on one stage make all that music? They absolutely blew me away. The member of the band that wowed me the most was the drummer, Neil Peart. The best way I could describe him is a drummer's drummer, meaning he has thousands of drummer fans who admire his playing. And he deserved all that praise because his drumming is next level.

That Rush concert helped me experience rhythm at a different level. It challenged what I even thought rhythm meant and felt to me. I love telling that story because I like to remind people that when we try to define something intangible like rhythm, words often fall short. What matters most is experiencing things and feeling them at a deep and personal level. Final note on Rush, even if you're not a progressive rock fan, watch a few live videos of Neil Peart, he was a legend for reason.

Interestingly, music therapist Destiny R. Boyum, MT-BC, shares that "when babies are in the womb, they're exposed to a heartbeat, the repetitive rhythm is a very natural thing." In addition to having already connected with our mother's heartbeat, rhythm is a key component in making and listening to music in just about every culture in the world. You can feel it deep in your soul, from the very first chords of a song to the moment the drums kick in. The rhythm of a piece of music is undeniable and something that is clearly being felt beneath the conscious surface.

In its simplest definition, rhythm is the relationship between the length of one note and another note. If I mention the song "Jingle Bells," the first thing that may come to mind is the iconic beginning rhythm: "jin-gle bells, jin-gle bells." Or put another way, the rhythm lengths of those first few notes are "short-short-long, short-short-long."

Beethoven's Fifth Symphony is another iconic rhythm that immediately lets us recognize the melody with just a few note rhythms: "ba-ba-ba-bum!" How is it that we can recognize these pieces of music with so few notes?

It's all in the rhythm.

That's why rhythmic activities like clapping, marching, and tapping along are so effective when learning music. It's not an optional part of music, but an integral part that cannot be separated. One cannot exist without the other. Without rhythms, notes would just ring forever and be quite lifeless. Our brains are perfectly suited to pick up rhythms and clap or tap along. According to Daniel Levitin in his book *This Is Your Brain on Music*, "the neural basis for this striking accuracy is probably in the cerebellum, which is believed to contain a system of timekeepers for our daily lives and to synchronize to the music we are hearing."

This is great news for you as a parent because you don't even have to "teach" your child how to find the beat and clap along; you simply need to demonstrate what you already naturally do when you listen to music.

While we're on the subject of rhythm, let me reiterate for those of you who may think that you have "no rhythm" that, statistically, it is so rare for someone to be rhythmically deaf that it's very, very, and I mean, very unlikely, so don't stress out about this. You have more than enough rhythm to instill it in your child. You can do this! One of the core beliefs at Color Me Mozart that we teach parents is that you can make rhythm a natural part of your child's routine, turning everyday moments into mini music lessons that build fluency and joy.

Music as Worship, Math, and Everything In-Between

In an email from Amanda, mom of three, she wrote me the most beautiful line: "We don't care if any of our kids become professional musicians. We just want them to carry music in their hearts the way we do, and pass it on to their own children one day."

In their homeschool, music isn't confined to a 30-minute slot. It's the calm classical playlist that settles everyone for morning lessons. It's the upbeat songs that turn chores into dance parties. It's the worship set that closes the day with raised hands and quiet tears. Some days they memorize math facts with silly songs. Other days they explore jazz to learn about the Harlem Renaissance.

Amanda and her husband, Jared, weave music into nearly every part of their children's day—so naturally that it never feels forced. On Sundays, Jared leads worship at their church, giving the kids one more living example of how deeply music matters to their parents.

At home, they often listen to anything from a symphony to a bluegrass session and talk about what colors it paints in their minds. Amanda says, "We're not teaching them to play an instrument as much as we're teaching them to feel the world more deeply."

That's the gift you're giving your children too. Not just notes on a page. A lifelong companion that helps them worship, wonder, work, and love, long after the last lesson is over. And one day, they'll thank you with a song.

■ Did You Know?

Rhythm Starts Before Birth
Seven-month-olds detect rhythmic patterns from womb exposure (Hannon et al., 2019). Your child is born ready!

Daily Rhythm Rituals: Clapping, Marching, and Tapping

Let's use a practical example with rhythm and clapping mentioned in the previous chapter. The song "If You're Happy and You Know It" is perfectly suited for an activity like this.

In case you forgot the lyrics, here they are:

> *If you're happy and you know it, clap your hands*
> *If you're happy and you know it, clap your hands*
> *If you're happy and you know it*
> *And you really want to show it*
> *If you're happy and you know it, clap your hands.*

In the following verses, replace "clap your hands" with "stomp your feet," "shout hurray," and finally "do all three." The great thing about a song like this is that it involves not only a recognizable rhythm, but also includes easy-to-follow movements. And don't forget, you don't need to stick to the same lyrics every time. Make up different lyrics and movements; kids' songs do this all the time. Instead of "clap your hands," you can say "pat your head" or "tap your knees." The important thing is to keep it fun and repeat these rhythms over and over.

These daily rhythm rituals are like the games I played with my sisters, mimicking the cadence of our parents' Spanish. They weren't always musical, but they taught me to feel patterns, just like clapping to a song. You can do the same with your child, making rhythm a playful routine that sticks.

■ Try This at Home

Rhythm Kitchen Jam

Grab spoons or pots and create a rhythm (e.g., tap-tap-pause-tap). Have your child copy it, then let them lead. Sing "If You're Happy and You Know It" while tapping. This builds rhythm and coordination while keeping it fun.

■ Parent Takeaway

In the beginning, you don't need to teach rhythm formally. Your child learns it by copying you. Clap, tap, or march together, and you're building their musical foundation.

Clapping Along With Songs

When I teach private lessons, I always share with parents small ways in which they can continue music education throughout the week, even when their child is not necessarily sitting at their instrument. Music, luckily, is all around us, pretty much 24/7. We don't have to go very far to run into a song playing or a beat being heard. Why not use those moments as mini music lessons?

Let's take a deeper dive into rhythm and how we, as adults, clap along to music. If you've been to a concert at any point in your life, you most certainly found yourself at some point bobbing your head, moving your shoulders, snapping your fingers, or clapping along.

NO RIGHT WAY, JUST YOUR WAY.

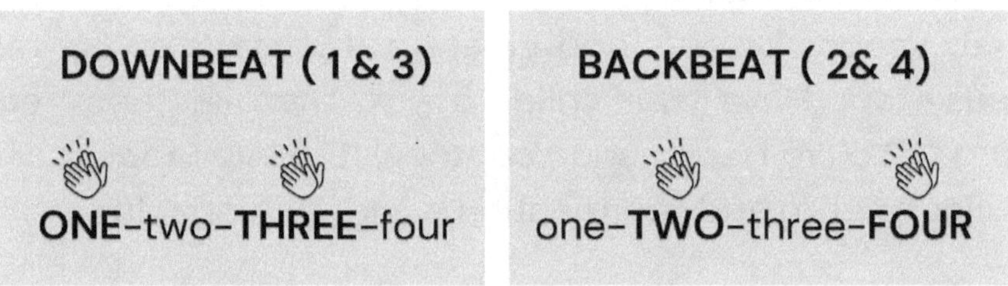

If you haven't yet done this, your homework is to put this book down and go buy tickets to your favorite band and go see them! You may not have instinctively known this, but depending on how you clapped along, it indicated how you naturally feel the beat when listening to music. Let me explain.

Most music, not all, but most, can be counted in groups of four beats. Basically, one-two-three-four, and then it repeats, one-two-three-four. Depending on where you clap, let's say you clap on beats two and four like this, one-TWO-three-FOUR, that shows that you feel the *backbeat* or *upbeat*. If you, however, clap on the one and three like this, ONE-two-THREE-four, then you feel the beat on the *downbeat*.

Keep in mind there is no right way to "feel" the music; it's just your personal way of interpreting what you hear. As mentioned in a previous chapter, the rhythms you heard as a young child had a big influence on what you naturally feel today.

■ Did You Know?

Rhythm Boosts Coordination

Clapping/marching improves motor timing and academics (Gordon et al., 2020). Rhythm = brain + body workout.

■ Parent Takeaway

Clapping to music is a natural instinct you already have. Share it with your child, and you're teaching them rhythm without even trying.

■ Try This at Home

Concert Clap-Along

Play a favorite song in the car and clap along on the "two and four" beats (one-TWO-three-FOUR). Invite your child to join, then switch to "one and three" (ONE-two-THREE-four). This teaches them to feel different beats playfully.

Integrating Beat into Everyday Life

As wonderful as this all sounds in theory, we have to somehow bring this into a practical application for everyday life. The good news is that music is already all around us; it's simply a matter of elevating those moments into something more.

In the next few pages, we'll look at some practical examples of how you can introduce concepts of rhythm into your child's life. You may even already do some of the activities we've already mentioned, like clapping along to songs or dancing. These are already great musical things to do, even if you weren't aware that you were, in fact, already deepening your child's understanding of rhythm.

A great place to start is by using songs that already incorporate movement in the lyrics. Take the song "Freeze Dance," for example. It is not only a catchy melody but also includes in the lyrics instructions on when to move, dance, twirl, and, most importantly for this song, freeze.

This is a great example of rhythm and timing being a primary force behind a song. Kids know exactly when to freeze and when to move. This develops and strengthens a child's inner rhythmic feel without consciously having to count beats or read music.

Below is a list of just a few of the hundreds of songs that combine movement and music:

- Freeze Dance
- If You're Happy and You Know It
- One Little Finger
- Ants Go Marching
- The Hokey Pokey
- Head, Shoulders, Knees, and Toes
- The Wheels on the Bus
- Going on a Bear Hunt
- Itsy Bitsy Spider

As with anything involving music or learning a new task, consistency is key, so make sure to incorporate music and movement often. In many cultures, dancing is inseparable from music. Where there is music, there is movement and dancing.

Unfortunately, here in the United States, we don't typically dance to music very often. We mostly just listen to it. But it doesn't have to be this way. If you encourage your child to move with music, they will develop a special connection with their own movements and the music they hear. This is a very special gift you can give them early on, even if it's something you may have not grown up with yourself.

If you are a person that struggles with dancing and feels bit silly, always remember that we were made to be moved both emotionally and physically by music.

One lovely side effect of introducing your child to beats and rhythms in their everyday lives is that your home will be filled with all kinds of incredible music. These are core memories that will be made simply by making the decision to have music be a central part of your family's everyday life. I have never met one parent who told me that they regret sharing too much music with their kids!

■ Try This at Home

Freeze Dance Party

Play "Freeze Dance" or another song from the list above. Dance with your child, freezing when the music stops. Let them choose when to pause the music. This builds rhythm, timing, and listening skills in a joyful way.

■ Parent Takeaway

Turn everyday moments into rhythm lessons by dancing or moving to music. It's a gift that fills your home with memories and music fluency.

Keep the Genres Coming

While we're on the subject of music in the home, I want to take a moment to remind you to not stick with just one style or genre of music. Admittedly, I have been guilty of this myself. I fall in love with a specific style of music and then only listen to that for a long time. There's almost a comfort in listening to the music we hear when we were young.

What I am asking you to do is to consciously fight against the urge to be a one-genre household.

In our earlier discussion about the importance of the rhythms we hear as children, we learned that it is critical to let your child listen to many different genres and styles of music. Remember that these are the rhythms they will feel most comfortable with for the rest of their lives. I didn't believe it either; however, it couldn't be more true.

Let's keep in mind that when we listen to music, different parts of our brain are engaged. For example, we may feel physiological responses from music, like an increased heart rate from the electrical activity in the brain. As you listen, the *auditory cortex* of the brain analyzes the pitch and volume of the song.

Then, the *amygdala* processes the emotions you feel in the moment, while the *mesolimbic system* manages pleasure responses by releasing neurotransmitters like dopamine.

Memory centers and motor systems also become active when we listen to music. This activation shows a strong connection between music, memory, and the impulse to move around, i.e., dance.

Additionally, music can influence our visual perception, affecting our perspective on the world. For example, in a study at Cambridge University, the psychology department had subjects listen to certain rap songs and found that their narratives were capable of evoking positive visual imagery, which could be helpful with mental health issues such as depression.

Different music genres and songs can evoke different responses in the brain as they activate specific neurons and unique memories and emotions. Your brain absorbs these new musical experiences and makes connections to the previous emotions created during a specific moment while listening to familiar music. The term neuroplasticity helps explain how this process works by showing how our brain changes and adapts when we experience new things.

> ***Neuroplasticity*** *is the ability of the brain to form and reorganize synaptic connections, especially in response to learning or experience.*

Listening to music is like tasting freshly cooked food. Music, much like cooking, offers a diverse palette of notes, instruments, and lyrics, conveying a unique style and creating different "dishes" with their own unique "tastes."

Just like a chef or a cook at home can experiment with new spices and ingredients to enhance their dishes, exposing one's ear or brain to these new ingredients [music genres] triggers distinct cognitive functions, leading to the opening up of new or enhanced perspectives. Adding new spices can transform a familiar dish into a completely new one, either inspired from past cooking, taste, and ingredients or brand new discoveries, and so can exposure to various musical genres expand one's emotional and cognitive palate, offering new and enhanced perspectives and insights.

■ Did You Know?

Variety Shapes Musical Flexibility
Diverse genres build auditory processing and flexibility (Trainor et al., 2016). Variety is key!

■ Parent Takeaway

Expose your child to a variety of music genres, just like you offer different foods. It builds a richer musical brain and opens new emotional worlds.

Feeling Music Before Labeling It

According to Susan Rogers, most toddlers can't resist the urge to march and clap to music, and this suggests that Homo sapiens are born with the neural infrastructure for extracting a subjective rhythm from regularly timed events. What this means for us non-neuroscientists is that our earliest years of development are a fertile time for hearing and internalizing rhythms.

You've probably heard a particular song having a certain "groove." But what exactly is a groove? Sure, we can count the beats of a song and even write out the rhythms in music notation, but groove is something that's beneath the surface.

Think about the difference between the words of a sentence and the deeper meaning that those words can have. Groove is that subjective part of music's rhythms that gets us to move, makes our heads bob, makes our bodies dance, and gets our feet tapping. This is something we are born with and happens way before we ever label it. In fact, if a person never becomes a musician or learns how to read music, they can still feel music as intensely as possible and connect with it at a very deep level.

When I was a teenager, and fell in love with music, I would go to just about every live concert I was able to. Whether it was live jazz, A Mozart Piano Concerto, Depeche Mode, or the Spin Doctors (I know this ages me), I would one hundred percent be locked into the rhythms and grooves of the night.

Seeing and hearing live musicians create a musical moment right in front of my eyes was intoxicating for me, and I wanted to experience it as much as I could. Although I had begun to

Whole Note
Lasts 4 beats (1-2-3-4)

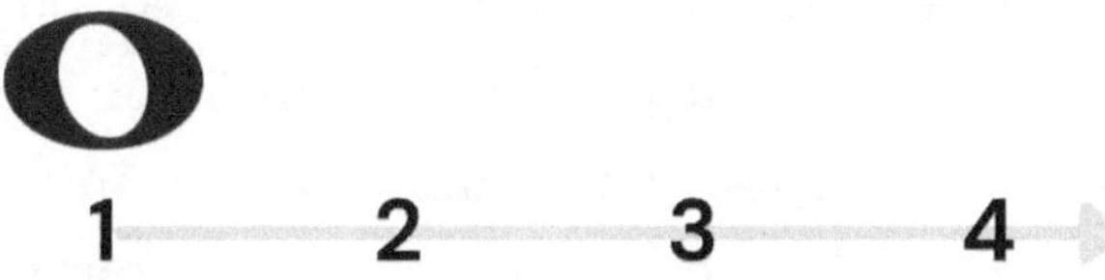

Try singing a note that lasts for 4 beats.
Hold it long and strong!

study music around that same time, I wasn't skilled enough in my music reading or theory to understand what many of those musicians were doing.

I simply felt it and didn't need the musical definitions of the chords, scales, or rhythms they were using to enjoy it any more than I already was. I knew that it was connecting to a deeper part of me, and the only thing I lamented was not finding music sooner in my life.

As the years passed and I became a professional musician and educator, I decided that I would make it my mission to help others connect with music at a deeper level. More specifically, I wanted to help parents be able to share this deeper level of music with their children, even they themselves were not musicians.

Let's try an exercise together. Think of a moment in your life where you were moved by a certain song or piece of music. Bring it to the foreground of your conscious mind and try to relive what that song makes you feel.What are you feeling? Is it joy? Nostalgia? Sadness? Happiness? Longing? The list of feelings can go on and on and is a testament to how deep in our minds and thoughts music can go.

Those feelings that come rushing back so quickly are a reminder of how important it is to have music be a part of your everyday life with your kids and family. We live in a time where we are inundated with so much content and entertainment that it's easy to believe that you should only play "kids' music" for your children. Nothing could be further from the truth.

When you read your child a book, you look for stories that carry with them a deep meaning. Perhaps a story with a moral lesson hidden beneath the rhymes and drawings. We want more for kids than just surface-level entertainment. When it comes to music, it's very much the same thing.

In addition to nursery rhymes, I strongly encourage you to play music for them that has more complex structures, deeper meanings, and a richer palette of instruments. These pieces will help them develop a better relationship with "groove" and "feel," even way before they learn what a *whole note* is. (A whole note is a note that lasts for four beats, by the way.)

If you don't know where to start on how to introduce your kids to different styles of music, I've prepared a list that will get you started. I do want to mention that this is by no means a definitive list (there isn't one), but merely a starting point to inspire you to listen outside of your comfort zone.

If you already play a healthy amount of different genres and rhythms in your home, congratulations, keep it up. For those seeking some guidance, get your list at: ColorMeMozart.com/rhythm.

■ Did You Know?

Music Sparks Emotional Depth

Complex music engages emotional centers, fostering empathy (Menon & Levitin, 2018). Deep music = deep bonds.

■ Chapter Recap

1. **Rhythm Is Natural**: Your child is born with the ability to feel rhythm, from their mother's heartbeat to iconic songs like "Jingle Bells."
2. **Daily Rituals Build Fluency**: Clapping, marching, and tapping to songs like "If You're Happy and You Know It" make rhythm a fun, natural part of life.
3. **Clapping Teaches Timing**: Clapping on different beats (e.g., two and four or one and three) helps kids feel music instinctively, no formal lessons needed.
4. **Integrate Rhythm Everywhere**: Songs with movement, like "Freeze Dance," turn daily routines into rhythm lessons, strengthening timing and coordination.
5. **Variety Fuels Growth**: Exposing kids to diverse genres shapes a flexible musical brain, opening emotional and cognitive worlds.
6. **Feel Before Labeling**: Kids connect to music's "groove" before understanding notation, making early exposure to rich music essential for lifelong connection.

Chapter 8

Music Literacy vs. Music Fluency

> *The only thing better than singing is more singing.*
>
> —Ella Fitzgerald

The terms fluency and literacy often get mixed together and can seem almost synonymous at times; however, they are quite different. While *fluency* can encompass speaking, reading, and writing a language, *literacy* directly refers solely to reading and writing. Being fluent in speaking a language is generally a prerequisite to becoming literate in it. We speak a language way before ever learning how to read and write it. We'll dive more into fluency in a moment.

When I grew up, as I mentioned in a previous chapter, there was very little written Spanish in our home. Even if there were any books lying around, obviously as an infant, I wouldn't have been able to make sense of those words for years to come. Rather, it was constantly hearing my parents speak to me and my sisters in Spanish that allowed me to gain fluency in those early years. Additionally, we would occasionally watch an Argentine or Latin television show, but even that was rather limited. The lion's share of my fluency in Spanish came from listening, feeling, processing, and responding to my parents.

What does that tell us about language acquisition in those early years? Basically, it points to the power that simply listening can have in the early development of a child. Even without formal education, our brains are ready to absorb language to listening in miraculous ways. That's why it's critical that parents and teachers make sure that children receive as much language as possible during those earliest years.

■ Did You Know?

Fluency Precedes Literacy

Oral fluency develops before reading (Goswami, 2017). Music follows the same path.

Fluency = Hearing, Feeling, and Responding to Music

According to Merriam-Webster, "fluent" is an adjective that describes being capable of using a language easily and accurately or effortlessly smooth and flowing.

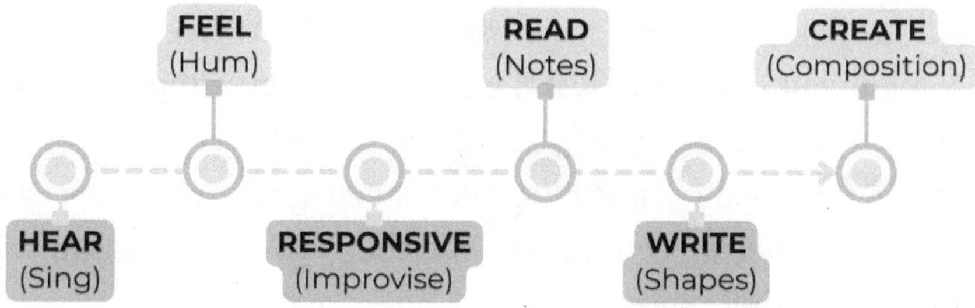

Now that we have a clear definition of what fluency in a language is, we can make the jump to imagine what it could look like with something like music. Assuming you are fluent in English if you are reading this book, I would imagine if we met and had a conversation, you would be able to express yourself quite articulately without the use of a dictionary or other grammatical aid.

In other words, you would be able to "improvise" words confidently and arrange them in any order to form sentences and phrases to express exactly what you're feeling. I could probably further assume that you wouldn't come with pre-scripted answers to read in case you get stuck during our conversation. These are things we don't think about very often, but it's quite fascinating just how fluent we are when it comes to our first language. Perhaps we even take it for granted, but we could easily talk for hours on end, continuing to connect thoughts in our minds with seemingly no end in sight. Our brain is the most efficient and largest hard drive ever. That is fluency at its best.

The incredible part is that, barring a particular developmental delay, most of us reach fluency while we're relatively young, continuing to deepen that fluency throughout our lives. And much like my Spanish, you didn't have to "try" to become fluent, it kind of just happened and never thought twice about it. You may give yourself a well-deserved round of applause for having learnt to speak a language fluently with ease. We may marvel at computers, but they have nothing on our brains' computing power!

■ Try This at Home

Sing and Respond Game

Sing a short phrase (e.g., "Twinkle, twinkle, little star") and have your child respond with their own made-up phrase. Take turns improvising. This builds music fluency by encouraging creative expression, like speaking a language.

■ Parent Takeaway

Fluency in music is about feeling and responding, not perfection. Your child can "speak" music naturally, just like they learned to talk, with your encouragement.

Fluency in Music

This is all great, but what does this have to do with learning and becoming fluent in music? Glad you asked. We can learn a lot by observing how we naturally learned language. We concluded that fluency began by simply hearing language from the earliest stages of life. What if we did this with music?

Now I don't want us to get confused. Simply having music playing in the background like some sort of soft soundtrack is not what I mean by mirroring language with music. Think about how we introduce language to kids in their first few years. We are relentless, providing language prompts and help from day one. Think of how many times you would talk, read, and annunciate words to your child. How many times you said, "ma-ma" and "pa-pa" over and over again.

How many times you pointed to something like a basketball and spoke what it was, hoping they would repeat it back to you. Endless amounts of words like clouds, ball, toy, horse, crayon, etc. It's a never-ending waterfall of language at every moment. In fact, the thought of having a silent house or not talking to your child for more than a few minutes is unfathomable. Think of all the storybooks you read to them, acting out every part of the story. Thousands of words a day being spoken directly to your child.

All of these actions essentially bring language to life, and you did it naturally because of your own fluency or "improvisational" skills with language. You never thought, "Can I do this?" You just did it with confidence and imparted fluency to your child. You did that! I'm here to share the great news that you can now do the same thing with fluency in music, regardless if you've never had so much as one music lesson. Fortunately, the ABCs of music are very similar to language and, in my opinion, even easier to learn.

When I first created Color Me Mozart, it was so that preschoolers could not only enjoy music and movement but also so that they would become literate in music. As time went on, I realized that it was parents who could truly benefit from these tools so that they in turn, could be their children's first and most influential music teacher. And much like the beginning stages of fluency with language needing no written word, we can also begin the first few years of music with no written musical notation as well. How do we do this? Let them listen to lots and lots of music.

Remember previously when I mentioned the term "cultural literacy" or being aware of different cultures? I want to apply that concept for a moment when it comes to the types of music that you let your child listen to. This involves nothing more than playing a wide variety of music in your home and, more importantly, being intentional about listening actively to it. Additionally, I recommend watching live recording of music as much as possible. With so many endless resources we have at our disposal today, you can watch real musicians create incredible music from all around the world.

I see families make time for tablets, cartoons, and movie night, but I don't see that much intentional music listening happening. Don't get me wrong, you don't need to sit your toddler down in front of a 45-minute Beethoven symphony (although that would be amazing). For instance, take a song they already know, like *Twinkle, Twinkle, Little Star*, and do a search for a 'live ukulele version'. Or maybe a tuba version (yes, that does exist, and it's awesome).

This provides a richer experience with music than they would otherwise have had. I'm not against pop music, songs on the radio, or music heard in cartoons. I've just witnessed that all too often, that it winds up being the only music that children are exposed to for most of their childhood. There's so much more to music, and you can be their first music teacher that lays the foundation for a lifetime of music fluency.

■ Did You Know?

Music Fluency Boosts Creativity
Improvisational music enhances divergent thinking (Sowden et al., 2019). Fluency fuels imagination.

■ Try This at Home

Musical Story Time
Play a short piece of music (e.g., a jazz tune or classical piece) and ask your child to make up a story about what they hear. This encourages active listening and builds music fluency through imagination.

■ Parent Takeaway

Be intentional about music, just like you are with language. Play diverse songs and engage your child actively to spark their musical fluency.

Literacy = Decoding and Performing from Notation

We've discussed at length the importance of fluency, not only for music, but in language as a whole. Using this experience in learning our native tongue, we can deduce that spoken language and fluency come first and naturally so since it is all around us.

We could also make the argument that spoken language is enough. After all, being able to communicate to the next generations is the goal of transferring knowledge, wisdom, and information.

This oral tradition of communication could be viewed as sufficient in order to allow the human race to continue, evolve, and express itself. However, it doesn't take long to see why this argument would fall apart rather quickly. When it comes to faithful reproduction of ideas, thoughts, and first-hand accounts, humans are historically unreliable in staying close to the source of the information.

Why we need notation.

Oral tradition distorts. Notation preserves.

Person 1: "Music is fun!"
↓
Person 2: "Music is run!"
↓
Person 3: "Moo sick is run!"
↓
Person 4: "????"

Think back to the first time you played the "telephone" game in school. If you've never played before, the rules are quite simple. You get a group of people in a room and whisper a sentence to the first person and then tell that person to whisper it to another until you reach the last person. It should be no surprise that by the time the phrase is reiterated by the last person, it is, if not completely different, at the very least, altered significantly.

This is because our brains, in order to save energy, try to focus on the most important parts of a sentence and drop the not-so-important details. On the surface, this seems like a good use of energy by the brain. After all, in an emergency, you really only need the essentials in order to survive.

However, when you're trying to convey an important message or idea across multiple people and generations, details most definitely matter, and that's where the brain's energy-saving plan doesn't work out so well. This is why we rely on the written word for just about every bit of information we wish to preserve in humanity. Things like recipes, history, science, math, religious texts, and of course, music are all written down in order to preserve as faithful a copy of the original creator's thoughts.

The interesting thing about the written word is that even if a hundred people read the same book, they can still extrapolate different meanings from it, and that yet is another reason we so desperately need ideas in written form.

■ Did You Know?

Notation Enhances Precision

Reading notation improves melody accuracy (Stewart et al., 2020). Notation = music's written record.

Decoding the Written Word

To move from the spoken word to the written word, we encounter a whole new set of skills and abilities that we must develop in order to use. Reading and writing now become a must in order to complete the circle of language and preserve its accuracy. In music, we face the same challenge. In the first few years of life, a child is exposed to an enormous amount of music.

In fact, a survey study of over 2,000 parents with children under three years of age in the United States reported that 60% of parents sang or played music to their child daily, while 92% did so on a weekly basis. An analysis of daylong audio recordings of infants found that music exposure made up about 9% of their day.

This is not an insignificant amount, and in the same way we move from spoken word to reading and writing, we also need to take this same approach when teaching kids music. Music composition has, in recent years, been relegated to an activity reserved for only the chosen few "talented" young musicians. This is, however, completely misguided.

Writing and composing music is no more difficult than creative writing in English class. Think of how early we start children with writing exercises. We encourage them to use their imagination and create their own stories, with their own worlds, using the words they have learned so far. It's the most natural thing in the world to encourage a child to do.

If we encourage, however, a child to "compose" music, I think you can imagine that the looks on people's faces would be one of confusion. Surely music composition must be taught in a conservatory? How could every child have the ability to write music? I'm here to tell you that they can and they will if you give them the opportunity!

We live in an ever-changing, fragmented, and niche-specific educational society. There is a club, league, camp, or study for anything and everything. This has proven at times to be a double-edged sword. When we break everything down into small niche areas of study, we lose the bleeding over of subjects into each other.

In the same way that learning to read is not merely the recitation of words on a paper, but is actually giving a child the tools to simultaneously express themselves in written form to the entire world and also be able to read the thoughts and ideas of any other human, whether they live today or lived a thousand years ago. That is the power of the written word.

With music, the effect is no less powerful. Using the smaller building blocks of music, we can begin to introduce the reading and writing of music to children in tandem with their ABCs. We can encourage them to create, play, and then write their own music. Imagine for a moment how much deeper their experience with music will be for the rest of their lives when they can participate in all facets of this language.

If you are not a musician, let me paint a picture in your own experience with language. I would bet that it would be hard for you to conceive what your life would even look like if you couldn't read or write but simply spoke a language fluently.

This is not to say you couldn't lead a normal life with only spoken word, but I doubt anyone would argue that the addition of literacy opens up worlds that would otherwise be off-limits. Let's not deprive children of this richness when it comes to music literacy.

From Exposure to "I Did It!"
A Mom in North Carolina

I still get emotional thinking about an email I received from a mom in North Carolina seven months after meeting her and her family at a homeschool convention. We spoke for quite some time and she decided to begin Color Me Mozart with her family.

Her seven-year-old twins both have developmental disabilities. In her message, she wrote that her goal was simply to provide exposure to music by leaving the books, flashcards, and a little xylophone out where her kids could touch them whenever they wanted. No lessons. No pressure. Just access.

For almost seven month, nothing obvious happened. Then one evening, one of her daughters sat down at the piano, opened the beginner book, and played straight through it. She looked up, eyes wide, and said, "Mom, the colors in the book are the same as the piano!" She ran to the xylophone and played the same songs there.

Color ➡ shape ➡ letter ➡ sound. The connection finally clicked. Her mom shared that she was crying as she typed: "It's helping her fine motor skills, her focus, everything. We're jumping for joy." She even added that she knew music would connect with her daughters, it was a matter of giving her enough time.

That's the magic of time and trust.

No pushing, no schedule, just a house filled with music and a parent who believed the breakthrough would come when her daughter was ready. And it did.

■ Try This at Home

Musical Echo Conversation

1. You sing a short, silly 3–4 note phrase (e.g., "Boo-boo-bee-bee" or any made-up tune).
2. Your child echoes it back as close as they can.
3. You echo whatever they just sang (even if it's different).
4. Keep the "conversation" going for 5–6 turns.

■ Parent Takeaway

Music literacy, like writing, lets your child create and share their own music. Start simple, and you're opening a world of expression.

Why We Need Both and How They Naturally Develop Together

So that brings us to the question, is fluency more important than literacy? Although we can argue that fluency is certainly a necessary precursor to literacy and can survive without it, ideally they work best together. Reverting to our comparison of musical fluency and literacy to language, our lives, it is safe to assume, were made better by the development of both.

More specifically, it was extremely effective to have learned literacy so soon after beginning to learn and gain fluency.

For most of us, we began learning the written word only a few years after we were born. I find it remarkable that even in these first years, we naturally, and correctly, assume that a child can handle and indeed thrive with learning the first building blocks of the written language. And I do believe this is instinctual.

When you consider the sheer number of languages and alphabets that exist in the world today and that a child born into that culture can almost certainly become fluent and literate is nothing short of a miracle.

How does a French child pick up French so perfectly? Or Mandarin? Or Tagalog? Hidden behind cartoons, nursery rhymes, coloring books, and simply speaking to a child is a complex neural development that would put a supercomputer to shame. In case you're wondering or curious like I was, according to Ethnologue, there are currently 7,164 living languages, and according to ScriptSource, 3,661 languages are known to be written. I don't know about you, but those statistics blew my mind.

And notwithstanding a developmental delay or other disability, any child born into any of those thousands of languages will become fluent in not too many years into their childhood. Isn't that incredible?

■ Did You Know?

Early Literacy Builds Confidence
Early notation boosts creative confidence (Hallam, 2016). Literacy empowers kids to create.

What This Means for Education

So great, a child can learn any language they are born into; how does that translate into music education? At the very least, it reframes the modern idea that music is only for the "talented" or those who can get private lessons. It also challenges our ideas of "confusing" a child with too much language. I can tell you that after years of meeting multilingual people from all over the world, the notion that a child would get confused learning more than one language at a time is a myth.

Don't ask me why this myth has taken such root in the past twenty years, but it has. Perhaps it has to do with our obsession with being hyper-focused on specific tasks and activities. Many of the families I work with run from one thing to another all week long. They see something like music as just another activity to be scheduled into their child's life.

I want to encourage you to begin thinking of music less as something to be "added" and something that you carry with you at all times, like you do speaking, reading, and writing. In this approach, music can follow a similar pattern of language learning, mainly, starting with fluency in listening, singing, and movement, and then continuing to the written form of music notation that will allow kids to compose and create their own music. This is not as crazy as you may think, especially if you are a parent who doesn't have any musical training under your belt.

Let me paint a different type of picture and ask if you feel you would be up to the challenge. Suppose you wanted to teach your child basic Spanish (if you're already a Spanish speaker, choose a different language). Do you think you could learn enough to teach them a basic sentence or two? Of course! My guess would be that you would look up basic phrases and words, practice them a bit, and then teach them to your child by repetition. That's the whole key to learning a new language right there. You already have the tools; it's a matter of using what you already know in your dominant language and applying it to the new one.

Your musical path will function exactly the same way. You won't start with a Mozart symphony or playing a Vivaldi concerto on the violin on day one. Instead, just as in the Spanish example, you will learn basic music concepts and melodic phrases, and then demonstrate those for your kids for them to learn from you.

As I mentioned earlier, modern thoughts about the difficulties of music education are flat-out wrong, and you can and should be your child's first music teacher.

■ Try This at Home

Music and Language Mash-Up
Teach your child a simple phrase in a new language (e.g., "hola" in Spanish) and pair it with a melody (e.g., sing "hola" to the tune of "Twinkle, Twinkle"). Then draw the melody as shapes on paper. This blends language and music fluency with literacy.

■ Parent Takeaway

You don't need to be a musician to teach music, just like you don't need to be a linguist to teach words. Start small, and you're giving your child a lifelong gift.

■ Chapter Recap

1. **Fluency Comes First**: Music fluency, like language, starts with hearing, feeling, and responding, not reading notes, and you can foster it naturally.
2. **Fluency Is Improvisation**: Just as you speak without a script, your child can "speak" music through singing and playing freely.
3. **Literacy Preserves Ideas**: Music notation, like writing, ensures accuracy and opens creative worlds, just as literacy does for language.
4. **Composition Is for Everyone**: Every child can compose music, just like they write stories, with simple tools and encouragement.
5. **Fluency and Literacy Work Together**: Early fluency through singing and movement paves the way for literacy, enriching your child's music experience.
6. **You Are the Key**: You have all you need to guide your child's music journey, starting with fluency and building toward literacy, no expertise required.

Chapter 9

The ABCs of Music: From Color to Notes

> *Children need the freedom and time to play. Play is not a luxury. Play is a necessity.*
>
> —Kay Redfield Jamison

As a preschool teacher, I was keenly aware that we were sometimes underestimating our students. Deep down, I knew that we could bump up students' music time into something deeper. So I began trying a few small musical experiments. Since we were already doing a lot of music and movement, namely singing and dancing, I wanted to see if we could get them to clap specific rhythms. As we discussed in chapter 6, this is an activity known as a *call-and-response*.

The method was simple enough. I would play a steady beat on a speaker, clap a rhythmic pattern and then motion students to try and clap the exact same rhythm back to me. And what do you know, they could do it! I did it again just to make sure it wasn't a fluke but again they clapped that rhythm right back at me perfectly. I then decided to take it a step further and make the rhythm progressively more and more complex until we hit a "wall."

I put that word in parentheses because I don't believe in educational walls, only a temporary marker for where we are in the present moment. It was, at least, their "wall" for now. What's great about an exercise like this is that you are merely demonstrating it for them, not doing it for them. This is another way we are mimicking language learning but applied to learning rhythm.

That simple experiment shaped how I approached teaching music, knowing kids could learn more than we often expect and give them credit for. At Color Me Mozart, we use simple, playful tools like colors and shapes to guide children from musical fluency to literacy, just as I did with my preschoolers.

■ Did You Know?

Kids Can Learn Complex Rhythms Early

Preschoolers imitate complex rhythms through playful repetition (Kirschner & Ilari, 2021). They're ready!

Using Color, Shape, and Play as Scaffolding

Since my students did such a great job with rhythm, I asked myself "how would they do with a simple melody?" My mind started racing and I got to work creating a way for them to be able to play a recognizable melody on an instrument. As I looked around the instruments in my office, I saw my piano, but decided that although a good choice, it would be cumbersome to move from student to student. Then my eyes landed on a colorful xylophone on my bookshelf and had a sneaking suspicion that it just might do the trick.

Observing that each note on the xylophone was a different color, I realized, with music having such a few notes as an alphabet, I could probably come up with a way to connect these colors to notes. After all, in order to play a melody, at its most basic level, you just have to hit the notes in the right order.

So I got to work, grabbed some colorful construction paper to match each note on the xylophone, laminated them, and then waited for my next music class. The first iteration of colors was as follows:

- Red = **C**
- Orange = **D**
- Yellow = **E**
- Green = **F**

- Light Blue = **G**
- Dark Blue = **A**
- Purple = **B**

The next class showed up, and I tried the first few notes of one of the simplest songs I could think of, *Mary Had a Little Lamb*. The great thing about that song is that, with one exception, it uses only three notes: C, D, and E.

This would be an ideal way to try my new system.

Before playing anything, we sang the song to make sure we had it fresh in our minds and voices. Next, I put the xylophone in front of one of my students, Sebastian, and handed him a mallet. I then proceeded to put the pieces of construction paper in the correct sequence in front of him.

For *Mary Had a Little Lamb*, with each note represented by a specific color, the first phrase looked a little like this:

Yellow(**E**), Orange(**D**), Red(**C**), Orange(**D**), Yellow(**E**), Yellow(**E**), Yellow(**E**)

Though that moment is one that left me speechless, I will attempt to describe what I felt when my student was able to play those notes in the right order. As Sebastian played the notes very slowly, carefully following each paper, there was a moment where it clicked, and you could see his eyes light up because he realized in that instant what he was playing. He was so proud of himself!

I'm not exactly sure who was smiling more, me or him, but it was a moment I will never forget. And just like that, I knew that we could indeed teach children how to learn and play music using the simplest form of language learning. I do want to remind us that just because something is simple doesn't mean it can't be used for profound learning. In fact, it's quite the opposite. Simple concepts allow us to begin learning everything in life, including language.

That is why, regardless of where a child is born, since they begin with simple concepts, they become fluent in their native language at a young age. Now we can do the same with music.

As we clapped and celebrated Sebastian's accomplishment with the xylophone, everyone wanted to be next.

My mind started to race after that, thinking, how far could I take this in a preschool classroom? Could I actually teach students how to read and play music at this age? I knew deep in my soul that it was possible, but I needed to get to work developing a system that could be easily understood by all children. Even more critical, I wanted to develop a music-learning system that teachers or parents with little or no musical knowledge could also learn and teach.

Remember that xylophone that I first used? There was something about it's color scheme that drove me a little crazy. It had two blues, a light blue and a dark blue. This made it difficult for kids to distinguish between notes.

After all, how light is light blue, and how dark is dark blue? And crayons and markers aren't any help since most packs don't include two different shades of blue. They do, however, include pink. Pink it is!

It was coming together. I had the beginnings of a system that would allow young children to play simple melodies that they already sang all the time. I was simply taking information they already knew and expanding on it.

Then I asked myself, "What else do kids know besides colors?" They know shapes too. And so shapes were added to each color. This would be the moment that I would use the pun, "it was starting to take shape," but I wouldn't dare.

This new updated notes represented by shapes and colors looked as follows: (Add shapes here)

- Red/Square = **C**
- Orange/Triangle = **D**
- Yellow/Circle = **E**
- Green/Diamond = **F**
- Blue/Oval = **G**
- Purple/Rectangle = **A**
- Pink/Star = **B**

One thing I was particularly excited about was being able to use knowledge that preschoolers were already learning in their other subjects. As an added bonus, I was able to provide parents and teachers a way to teach music that was easy enough to understand regardless of their musical experience.

■ Try This at Home

Color Note Game

- Get a toy xylophone or use colored stickers on a keyboard. Assign colors to notes (e.g., red = C, yellow = E).
- Sing *Mary Had a Little Lamb* and place colored paper in order (yellow, orange, red, orange, yellow, yellow, yellow).
- Have your child play it. This builds fluency and introduces literacy playfully.
- For a free set of piano stickers, visit: ColorMeMozart.com/first-lesson

■ Parent Takeaway

Colors and shapes make music accessible. You don't need to read music to guide your child, just use familiar tools like a game.

Mimicking How Kids Learn Letters (Colors = Sounds, Shapes = Structure)

We've all heard the question, "If you could have one superpower, what would it be?" I know we usually go straight to flying or super strength, but what if we've been leaving a more practical superpower on the table this whole time? Namely, the superpower of learning different languages.

The moment I discovered I could connect something as simple as colors and shapes to musical notes on an instrument, I knew the next step was to create a bridge between fluency and literacy in music in a way that was easily understood and, more importantly, replicable in any setting.

Once again, I took my cues from how we learn language. When we learn language, we listen first, then we repeat back, and then progressively we gain literacy and learn how to read and write. The cycle by then is complete. One thing I was certain of was that I couldn't simply go from a shape or a color representing a note to straight into traditional music notation. There would have to be more nuance than that.

Instead, following more clues left behind by language acquisition, I concluded that there needed to be a few extra steps before we reached the ability to read music notation.

To quickly define the term, *music notation* is simply the written symbols and markings that you think of when you think of written music as in the example below (figure 9.1).

Let's take a trip down memory lane and try to remember our first encounters with the written word. More specifically, try to remember attempting to draw your first few letters. Although it will vary for everyone, we generally start trying to draw some type of letter between the ages of 3 to 5.

However, we don't dive straight into drawing letters or numbers. We first need more basic elements to work with. If we think of the steps needed to draw any letter or number, it will typically involve a set of lines and/or curves. Once we can draw a few of those, we can begin tackling letters.

Keep in mind that by this age, a child is generally already fluent and has been speaking the words that they are now trying to read and write. With counting, we start even younger, as early as two years old.

As children progress, they take these lines and curves and arrange them in a specific pattern to form a letter or number. Assuming a child is trying to draw the number "1," we would instruct them to draw a straight line straight down. Voilà, their first number and writing success!

This is indeed a big moment in our early developmental years, and it begins a momentum that, fortunately for us, travels with us our entire lives. I often feel that we don't stop often enough to consider how powerful learning how to read and write truly is. It is unfortunately one of those things that we do so naturally, we tend to take for granted.

To recap, when it comes to transitioning from fluency in language to literacy, we begin with the most basic geometric segments possible, arrange them accordingly, and then associate them with the words we already speak.

Using this as a blueprint for learning music, we can almost replicate it to a tee. As we've discussed earlier, we've already been listening to and interacting with music from inside the womb, and by the time we reach the age of four, we have heard hundreds and hundreds of pieces of music and songs. That is a lot of exposure to a "language" to simply leave it undeveloped. It would be a shame to not develop it further to gain both literacy and fluency.

Since music has an additional element of instruments, I knew this new system from basic shapes and colors to music notation also needed to include the ability to learn how to play an instrument.

And so, with all of that in mind, combined with my experience in early childhood development, I created the following system to take a child from knowing basic shapes and colors to being able to play an instrument and being fluent in the language of music:

The four levels of Color Me Mozart™

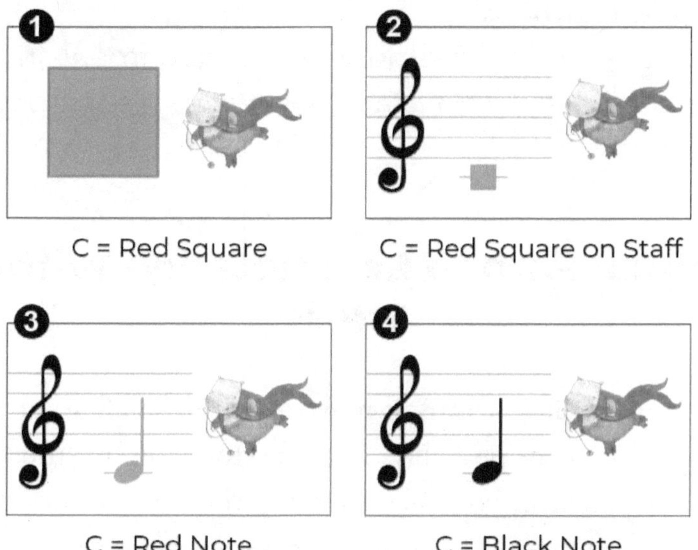

C = Red Square

C = Red Square on Staff

C = Red Note

C = Black Note

- **Level 1**: A note is represented by a shape and color (e.g., red square = C). The xylophone's red bar or a piano's red sticker is C, making it easy for parent and child to play.
- **Level 2**: Introduce staff lines with shapes placed on them, mimicking note placement on a musical staff while retaining the shapes and colors as notes.
- **Level 3**: Transition to traditional music notation, replacing shapes with standard note symbols while keeping color cues.
- **Level 4**: Transition to complete black and white music notation, removing all colors cues.

■ Did You Know?

Colors Aid Learning
Color-coding boosts memory and engagement in young learners (Dzulkifli & Mustafar, 2018). Colors = superpower.

Gradual Path to Real Notation Without Stress

If you think back to learning how to write your first letters and numbers, you can probably imagine the feel of the crayon, marker, or pencil in your hand tracing the dotted lines to form these new symbols. I could even remember how they smelled. Perhaps your memory floods with memories of the following types of worksheets:

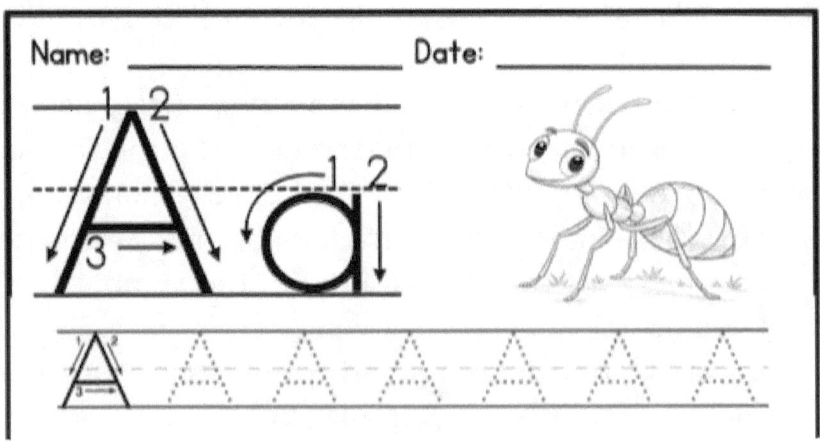

I can still remember how excited I got whenever we were given these types of sheets to work on in kindergarten. There was something so enjoyable about following the patterns and trying to make my letter A's look like the example. Mine were never quite so neat, but the challenge was always fun, and I couldn't wait for the next one.

I find it curious that such a mundane and repetitious task could be so enjoyable. If I had to analyze why it didn't seem boring at the time, it was probably because the task was hidden behind a seemingly "fun" activity.

Let's analyze some of the elements in this seemingly simple worksheet an what makes it so effective. First we have a fun and playful image of an ant, which reinforces the letter "A", helping a child associate it with something they most likely already know. Additionally, there is the added bonus of being able to draw and use markers or crayons, an activity in and of itself something that kids love doing. Finally, there is a repetitious element to it all. It's not a "once and done" activity, rather, it hides repetition in the activity itself to solidify its effectiveness.

If my teacher had said, "Today we will be practicing our penmanship in the hopes that one day you will gain the ability to proficiently read and write," I think I would have zoned out.

Fortunately, learning to write letters was actually fun, and as I observe other students at this stage of their education, more often than not, they also enjoy practicing drawing these new shapes called "letters." What if we turned learning music notation into the same type of experience?

Imagine how many children would be fluent and literate in music with almost no extra effort at all. And if your first thought is that it would be too much to put on a child, I only ask that you think back and remember if you felt overburdened in learning how to read and write your native language. My guess is that weren't overwhelmed at all.

■ Try This at Home

Trace the Treble Clef

Draw a large treble clef on paper (find a template at ColorMeMozart.com/worksheets). Have your child trace it with crayons, then color it. Sing a song while tracing to connect music and fun. This introduces notation like tracing letters.

■ Parent Takeaway

Tracing music symbols, like letters, makes literacy fun and natural. Your child can learn notation as easily as they learned the alphabet.

One Activity at a Time

This is why we've made a concerted effort to recreate the experience of these types of worksheets that use coloring and drawing to teach language in a setting for music education.

What I desperately didn't want was a watered-down version of music. In modern society, we are already surrounded by so much edutainment that promises to teach but fails to deliver. I wanted a real music education solution that was actually fun for parent and child, not more empty entertainment.

I wanted to follow the exact steps of language acquisition that already work so well and use them as a framework for music. When it comes to learning in a fun way, we hear both the term "gamify" and "edutainment" used quite often now; however, these concepts date further back than we imagine.

The idea of making learning fun and bite-sized and actually entertaining is not new and it's how we all approach teaching young children. Whether it's hiding a moral inside of a story or fable or teaching principles like teamwork while playing a silly game or sport, the use of entertaining educative activities is as old as humanity itself. It comes completely naturally to all of us and is a great way to learn.

Applying this same concept to our goal of musical fluency and literacy, we have produced activities and worksheets that mimic those of learning language.

In the example below, let's try to trace a musical symbol known as the *Treble Clef*. Even if you've never drawn a treble clef before, you'll have a lot of fun tracing the ones above, I promise. Note: freehand ones are a bit trickier, but give it a try!

And just as in tracing letters, we want to eventually be able to draw freehand, so we slowly wean off the tracing worksheets, moving closer and closer to music literacy. As a child progresses through their educational career, we are confident that they will master language literacy and be limited only by their own imagination. This too, is our goal with music. To give each child that same freedom of expression when it comes to music. Imagine a world where being able to read, write, and play music is as common as knowing your first language.

■ Did You Know?

Playful Learning Lasts
Game-based activities strengthen long-term skill retention (Pyle et al., 2020). Fun works.

■ Chapter Recap

1. **Kids Are Ready for More**: Children can learn complex rhythms and melodies early, just like they learn language, with playful tools like colors and shapes.
2. **Colors and Shapes Bridge Fluency to Literacy**: Using familiar tools like colors (e.g., red = C) and shapes (e.g., square = C) makes music accessible to kids and parents.
3. **Scaffolding Mimics Language**: Gradual steps from colors to notation mirror how kids learn letters, building fluency and literacy together.
4. **Play Makes It Fun**: Tracing music symbols, like tracing letters, turns literacy into an engaging game, not a chore.
5. **No Music Experience Needed**: Parents and teachers can use Color Me Mozart's system to teach music, just as they teach the alphabet, with no prior knowledge.
6. **A Lifelong Gift**: Teaching kids to read, write, and play music gives them the same expressive freedom as language literacy.

Chapter 10

Music as Family Glue: Reclaiming Shared Music in a Digital Age

> *To teach a child to play an instrument is to teach him to speak a second language.*
>
> —Shinichi Suzuki

A hundred years ago, if you wanted to listen to music in your home, someone had to physically create it. A parent, a grandparent, an older sibling, someone sat at the piano, picked up the guitar, or started singing a song while getting ready for dinner. Music wasn't consumed. It was created, together.

Fast-forward to today: we have every song ever recorded in our pocket… and yet most of us listen to music in solitude, in the car, on headphones, or during workouts. Even music lessons have unfortunately followed the same pattern: drop the child at the teacher's studio, wait in the car, pick them up 30 minutes later. In essence, music, the greatest unifier in human history, has quietly become one more individual activity.

But it doesn't have to be this way.

What if we pressed rewind when it comes to musical experience in our homes? What if we put down the headphones, picked up instruments, and created music together, as families? I not only believe this is possible, but I truly feel this is something that is urgent and must be done in order to reverse the unfortunate direction of music having flowed from a communal experience to one that is very individualized.

One of the core beliefs we have at Color Me Mozart isn't just that kids learn notes and rhythms early but that the living room becomes the classroom, the kitchen table becomes the stage, and the parent, most importantly, becomes a band member.

You're not outsourcing music; you're reclaiming it as the family ritual it was always meant to be. When you sing "Itsy Bitsy Spider" together at bath time, clap rhythms over dinner, or turn pots and pans into a band, you're doing more than teaching music. You're doing what families did for centuries: using sound to say "we belong to each other."

Technology gave us infinite music. You get to decide whether it divides the family… or brings it closer. Make the choice your great-grandparents never had to make. In fact, keep Spotify, keep YouTube, keep the convenience, but bring the music back home, back to shared voices, shared laughter, shared air.

That's the real revolution.

The Garcia Family Band

The Garcias had three kids under six and constant chaos.

Mom, Laura, once told me, "We love each other, but the kids fight a lot and don't have activities that they can share together." I suggested one rule: Friday pizza night becomes music night. No screens, just instruments that were in the house, pots, spoons, shakers, pillows, and one song they all pick.

First week: disaster. Everyone shouted over each other. By week four they invented "The Pizza Song" with verses about toppings. By week eight the oldest was leading, the middle one kept perfect rhythm on a pot, and the toddler danced in circles.

A year later Laura sent a photo: all five of them singing on the porch with makeshift instruments, laughing and creating memories together. She wrote, "Music didn't fix everything, but it gave us a place to be on the same team again."

That's the magic you get to create in your own living room, no studio required.

Love as a teaching method

In her book *Love to Learn*, Isabelle Hau speaks about the importance of teaching with love. Multiple studies appear to show that development in young children can even be negatively affected if their educational experiences are devoid of love, care, and close relationships.

As parents, you have the unique opportunity to keep relational learning, or to use a term from Ms. Hau's book, Relational Pedagogy, as the central method for teaching your children. This invites all the added benefits that a loving and relational approach can bring to the educational experience of a young child, benefits that will have rippling effects into their adult lives. As Ms. Hau explains:

> *Love is a driving force that fosters connection, attachment, understanding, learning, and growth. When educators approach teaching with a focus on love, they create a fertile environment for holistic development, one where little learners are valued, understood, and more deeply engaged.*

She goes on to explain that compassionate pedagogy doesn't just emphasize academic success but cultivates relationships, emotional intelligence, and resilience, which are essential qualities for thriving in all areas of life.

I think there is so much we can learn from this idea of relational pedagogy. In fact, I believe that this concept comes quite naturally to parents who want to see their children thrive. Most parents would agree that in addition to desiring academic success for their children, just as importantly, they want to see them thriving in all areas of life.

Music is unique in that it brings with it a suitcase of feelings, emotions, memories, sensibilities, and love. If we were discussing mathematics, perhaps we would have a bigger challenge in adding the element of love and relational teaching to such a subject, however powerful it would be.

With music, on the other hand, love and compassion seem to be intricately intertwined already in the fabric of the subject itself. Music already has an emotional connection that just about everyone can identify with. The next logical step is to share those emotional connections with music with your kids. The science proves that if we give importance to the relational moments of learning, children benefit in all areas. This should be our ultimate goal.

This brings us back to our observations of how our musical experience has changed over the years—from being a communal experience to more of an individual one. Of course, many of us go to live concerts and share moments together while listening to music, or even at church where we sing together, but those are the exception and not the norm.

If we take a step back and observe how music is typically heard and consumed in this digital age, we quickly realize that it is delivered in small bits. Far from the days of a fifty-minute symphony by Beethoven, we now experience music minutes, if not seconds at a time. This has certainly had a significant impact on how we experience music together as a family.

Have you tried getting a toddler to sit through more than a few seconds of a music performance without fidgeting? Some may say that it's par for the course in a young child. However, if you place that same child in front of a quickly edited animation with tons of stimulation, that same child, who wouldn't sit still for ten seconds of music, will have no trouble sitting for the animation.

Is the animation at fault? Of course not. The main issue lies deep in how we've transformed our view of music and its role in the development of a child. From their earliest moments, infants are overstimulated and then become restless when that level of stimulation is removed. All we need is a reset in how we view music education and how we introduce it to our families, to maximize the myriad benefits that only music can bring to a young child. We need to interrupt the overstimulation of the digital world.

Reuniting the Family Through Music

All these ideas and philosophies may sound interesting, but at the end of the day, what we need are practical solutions in a heavily electronic world.

If you imagine in your mind a modern-day family doing an activity together, you might conjure up images of a family at an amusement park, watching television together, or even sitting at the dinner table. We don't generally imagine a family making music together.

On social media, there are many families that have become rather well known for forming a "family band." Unfortunately, we tend to see this as a novelty. We view them as a "talented" family. "We could never be like them," you may think to yourself —when in reality, if you replaced the occasional movie you would watch as a family with music time, you can easily bring music right back into your home.

Instead of trying to replace every ounce of entertainment with a learning moment, you can begin by substituting small moments here and there. For instance, say you are about to hand your little one a screen to keep them occupied. What if, instead, you use that same screen to watch a live music performance together of a song they love?

Many of my students love movies like *Star Wars*, *Bluey*, or *Mario Bros.* Instead of trying to convince them that Chopin's Piano Concerto No. 2 in F minor is the greatest piece of music ever written (yes, it's my favorite), I teach them music through songs they already love. You wouldn't believe how many versions of *Star Wars* there are out there. From the tuba to the ukulele, there are countless live versions of great musicians playing these iconic melodies.

Most importantly, kids are drawn in because they connect with those melodies. And the best part is that the rules of music can be taught the same way whether it's through Chopin or "Baby Shark."

■ Chapter Recap

1. **Music Was Once Family Glue:** A century ago, music was created together, sung, played, and shared in the home.
2. **Technology Turned It Solo:** Today, we have infinite songs in our pockets... but most of us listen alone.
3. **You Can Reclaim It:** Put down the headphones and pick up pots, spoons, voices, turn the living room into the stage.
4. **Shared Moments Build Bonds:** Singing at bath time, clapping over dinner, jamming in the kitchen says "we are a family."
5. **Small Rituals Create Big Memories:** One pizza-night band, one lullaby duet, one silly dance party at a time.
6. **No Studio Required:** In a digital world that often divides, music can reunite your family, starting tonight.
7. **Your Home Is the Classroom:** You're not just teaching notes, you're teaching love, connection, and joy.

Chapter 11

Turning Play into Practice (without pressure)

> *Music is too important to be left to the musicians.*
>
> —Claude Debussy

If you're anything like me, you can most likely recall many melodies from when you were a kid. Perhaps a song pops up on your playlist that you haven't heard for years, and you instantly remember all the lyrics. Even you're amazed at how you so quickly remembered all those lyrics without thinking twice. That's the power of music and how deeply it rests in our subconscious. It is literally a part of us and our long-term memory.

If you've ever had trouble memorizing something in particular, you probably have memories of a teacher or parent sharing a fun little tune to sing in order to memorize it more easily. A song that comes to mind for memorizing the names of countries, for instance, is called *Nations of the World* from the cartoon, Animaniacs, definitely worth a listen.

One of the earliest known examples of using music to aid memorization is the Alphabet Song, or the ABCs. We don't tend to give it much thought, but just imagine for a moment if we had to memorize twenty-six different symbols in a particular order and then recite them back in that same order. How long do you think it would take you, as an adult, to do something like that? I know for me, it would be an extremely challenging, if not impossible thing for me to do in a short mount of time.

But when it came to learning the twenty-six letters of our alphabet growing up, it was made possible, in part, by the use of music to make memorization much simpler. Here are some fun facts and history of the famous melody we all know and love. The *ABC Song* is composed of a French melody from 1761, which was paired with the alphabet lyrics by Charles Bradlee in 1835 when he copyrighted the work in the United States. The song has been in continuous use for nearly 200 years to teach the English alphabet to children. Bonus fun fact: It's the same melody as *Twinkle, Twinkle, Little Star*!

The reason this approach of mixing music with learning works so well is because music can utilize extra areas of the brain that language alone cannot. This is precisely why, when we teach young children music, we want to make sure to combine new music concepts, habits, and teachings with games that incorporate those elements.

I attempted to look up the statistics of how many times a child sings the ABCs by the time he or she is five years old, however I didn't find any reliable information. Perhaps it's not something that gets counted or analyzed; however, I truly feel it must be a very high number, most likely in the thousands.

Think of the amount of times you sat watching an ABC video with your kids or sang it together with them. Surely, we are looking at a substantial number. The reason this is important is because it shows that whenever we are learning anything new, at any age for that matter, repetition is a key factor.

Making learning fun is crucial in not having it feel like a chore. I'm sure if I asked you if you felt that singing the ABCs with your child was a chore, you would emphatically answer "not at all". In fact, it's safe to say you enjoy those moments immensely between you and your kids. That is because you turned education into play and praise. This is where we always want to be when it comes to early education.

■ Did You Know?

Music Enhances Memory
Songs activate multiple brain areas for better recall (Ferreri et al., 2019). Learning sticks!

Making Music Habits Stick with Games and Praise

As we progress beyond the ABCs and enter the realm of music education, we need to be more intentional because the systems may not already be in place for music the way they are set up for language. When it comes to language learning, everywhere you turn, whether it is YouTube, children's books, Disney, Sesame Street, or Bluey, you find language learning as part of the "entertainment." For music education, this isn't as ubiquitous.

By making music a playful part of your daily routine, you can replicate the effortless way kids learn language. In my preschool classes, I saw kids light up when we turned rhythm clapping into a game, not a lesson. The praise they got for trying kept them eager to continue. You can do the same at home, using games and encouragement to build music habits that last.

■ Try This at Home

ABC Song Remix

Sing the *ABC Song* with your child, adding claps or taps on each letter. Then try it faster or with silly voices. Praise their effort, not perfection. This makes music practice fun and memorable.

■ Parent Takeaway

Turn music into a game with praise, and it becomes a habit your child loves, just like singing the ABCs.

Music in Everyday Life

If you can't find early music education resources for young children readily available for parents to teach, what can you do to make sure your child is receiving ample music exposure in their first few years, even before their first lesson? Or even your first lesson?

Let's take a look at some of the foundational basics of music every child should be exposed to in their first few years. For some families, this will be a part of everyday life; for others, not so much. It is important to see what is perhaps missing musically from your home from the list below and begin to add it gradually.

One note before we dive in: be sure to keep these ideas fun and not as a checklist to be "finished." Just as with language, there is no finish line; there is the journey that makes it special and worthwhile. As I've shared with so many people before, I have never met parents who said, "Oh, I wish we didn't do so much music in our house!" There can never be enough, so enjoy each season as much as you can; your kids and you will remember it forever.

Everyday Music Activities

- **Sing Daily**: Sing lullabies, nursery rhymes, or made-up songs during routines like bedtime or bath time.
- **Move to Music**: Dance or clap to songs like *The Wheels on the Bus* to build rhythm and coordination.
- **Explore Instruments**: Let your child tap on a toy xylophone or bang on pots to discover sounds.
- **Listen Actively**: Play diverse genres (e.g., classical, jazz, folk) and talk about what you hear ("What's that sound like?").
- **Improvise Together**: Make up silly songs about your day, encouraging your child to add their own words or sounds.

■ Did You Know?

Playful Music Boosts Engagement

A 2020 study showed that playful music activities, like singing or dancing, increase children's engagement and motivation to learn. Fun keeps them hooked! (Source: Pyle, A., *Early Childhood Research Quarterly*).

■ Try This at Home

Kitchen Band

Use pots, spoons, or a toy xylophone to create a family "band." Take turns making up rhythms or melodies. Keep it silly and praise everyone's contribution. This builds music into daily life.

■ Parent Takeaway

Make music a fun part of your routine, like storytelling. It's not about perfection—it's about creating joyful memories.

The Progression from Toddler to Young Reader

If we were to boil down the goal of any educational endeavor, at the heart of it, we would see that mastery per se isn't the exact goal. Even in our adult lives, whenever we embark on a journey to learn a new skill, what we want to essentially see is progress.

Progress, simply put, is becoming better at something as time passes. If you are a little bit better at something today than yesterday, you feel motivated to keep going and continue to strive for progress.

I've heard it said before that it doesn't matter whether you are progressing from one to two or a million to two million; progress is all that matters. In my own experience in learning new things, I can attest to this being true in my own life.

The amount of progress is relative to what you knew before. The only true enemy to progress is stagnation. Whenever we exert energy and effort toward a goal and feel like we are in the same place as we were before, this makes us feel deflated and discouraged, making it more and more difficult to want to continue the pursuit of whatever goal we are striving for.

This is why practically all goal-achieving books recommend breaking big goals into small, more manageable steps that can be accomplished day by day. This increases the chances of accomplishing these smaller goals and keeps you feeling progress, motivating you to keep going.

The next time you watch a movie, see a great example of architecture or engineering, or listen to a beautiful symphony, keep in mind that it was all done accomplishing small steps towards a big goal. It's a simple principle that is behind the biggest ideas humanity has ever seen.

■ Did You Know?

Small Steps Drive Progress
Breaking skills into tiny wins fuels persistence (McPherson & Renwick, 2018). Progress feels good.

A Lesson From Star Wars

After reading that title, you're probably wondering, "what does *Star Wars* have to do with any of this?"

I promise it's not random. In fact, I hope it fascinates you as much as it did me. When I was a teenager, visiting a friend's house, I stumbled upon a book about the making of *Star Wars*. As I flipped through the pages, one image stopped me cold: the filming schedule.

Having never been on a film set before and it being before the time of 'behind-the-scenes' extras on movies, I actually had no clue how they filmed, let alone organized a movie production. It gave me a new found appreciation for how much work it actually takes to create and produce a movie, especially a masterpiece like Star Wars.

What struck me immediately was the level of detail of the filming schedule. It broke down every scene into tiny, manageable tasks such as lighting, costumes, sound, cameras, all planned meticulously. This wasn't about rushing to create a masterpiece; it was about small, deliberate steps that built something extraordinary.

That's how you can approach music with your child: break it into playful, bite-sized moments, and the progress will feel like magic. Even better, the result will actually be a masterpiece since you will be giving them the gift of music for a lifetime. Star Wars can't even compete with that!

■ Try This at Home

Progress Jar

Create a "music jar" where you add a colorful bead every time your child sings, plays, or tries a music activity. Celebrate small wins weekly. This shows progress visually and keeps motivation high.

■ Parent Takeaway

Focus on small, fun music moments, not mastery. Like a *Star Wars* film schedule, little steps lead to big results.

Examples of How Learning to Read Music Evolves Naturally at Home

We've already spoken at length about the accepted natural progression of language and reading in modern education. A child, in their earliest years, listens to their native tongue being spoken at home and gradually begins to repeat simple sounds, eventually evolving into complex phrases and fluency.

Typically, even before any type of formal schooling begins, whether in a school or at home, a child will begin to be instructed on how to recognize letters and connect them to the language they already speak.

If you step back for a moment and simply marvel at what happens in a child's early years of language acquisition, it's rather remarkable. Without necessarily any formal training, parents become their children's first and most important teacher when it comes to language learning. Most, if not all, fluency comes directly from parental demonstration, direction, and encouragement. I still find this to be an incredible feat, both by your role as a parent but also the mechanisms of the brain that allow this to even happen. This is the same roadmap you want to utilize at home with kids when it comes to music fluency and literacy.

Take, for example, the first time you try to explain to your child the letter "A." First, you sound it out with a long "aye" or short "ah" phonetic pronunciation so they can relate the sound of the letter with what they are seeing in written form. We know as adults that not all A's sound the same; however, we would never bombard a child with all the rules from the start.

We very naturally and strategically want a child to associate the written symbol with a sound they are hearing. We may even begin with a first word and object association, such as "A as in Apple." Now we have four connections that we are asking a very young child to do. Without realizing it, we are asking them to associate a sound they've heard but never read before with a written symbol and now a word and pronunciation all at the same time. I'd say that's some next-level computing by a child's brain!

What I really want you to take away from this particular example is that at no point in teaching your child to associate a letter with a sound or word or object did you feel you were overwhelming them. Instead, I can guarantee you felt you were doing what was completely natural and most beneficial to them. Great, now let's do that with music.

English Alphabet: 26 Letters
Musical Alphabet: 7 Letters

The great news is that we don't have twenty-six letters in the musical alphabet but only seven, and only twelve notes overall, so this is going to be way easier than teaching them how to read English.

■ Did You Know?

Music's Alphabet Is Simpler

A 2017 study noted that music's seven-note alphabet (A–G) is easier for children to learn than language alphabets, making early music literacy accessible. Music is simpler than you think! (Source: Patel, A. D., *Music, Language, and the Brain*).

Unused Piano Sitting in Your Home?

While not every home has a piano in it, statistics show that approximately 51% of American homes have some type of instrument. That's a lot of instruments. This means that if you're reading this book, there is a fifty percent chance that there is a piano, keyboard, guitar, or perhaps even drums sitting in some room or closet in your house.

I want to challenge you to do something for your kids. If you have a melodic instrument, meaning something like a guitar or piano/keyboard, take it out, dust it off, plug it in if needed, and put it somewhere that is out in the open and visible to the whole family.

Quick note for any guitars that are being brought out of the closet: take the extra step and tune it beforehand. There are plenty of great how-to videos available online that will help you do that in a minute or two. It's easier than you would think, trust me.

If you do have a piano or keyboard, follow the following instructions and charts below to locate a "C" key on your piano.

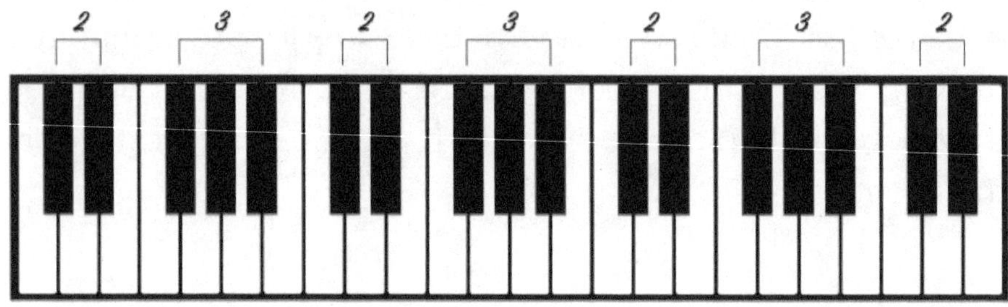

The first thing you'll notice is that your piano's black keys are arranged in groups of two, then three, then two, then three, and so on. The great thing about music in general is that it is structured in very logical and easy to recognize patterns. What you are looking at is not a hundred different notes, but the same notes repeated over and over, making them easy to identify.

Next, locate any set of two black keys. The white key directly to the left of those two black keys is a "C." Now you can play all the C's on the piano! See the chart below.

Now, I feel fairly confident that even if you've never had a single piano lesson in your life, you were still able to find all the C's on your piano. Keep in mind that depending on the size of your piano or keyboard, you may have a few more or a few less C's, but the important thing is that you can find identify them all.

The best part is that now you can teach and demonstrate that to your child. In the same way we associated the letter "A" with a

Finding all the C's on the Piano

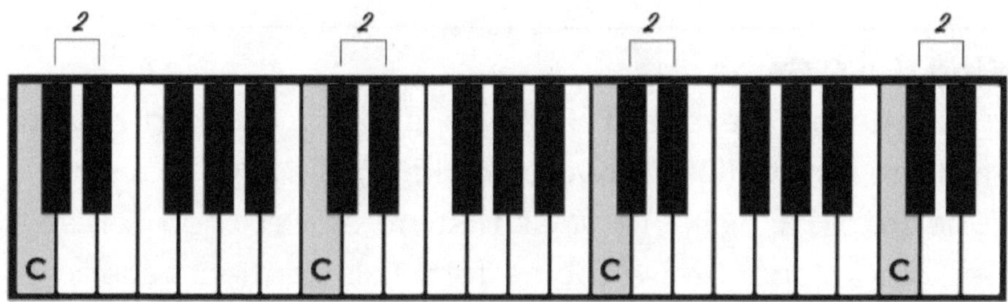

sound, word, and written symbol, now you can associate the note "C" with a key and sound on the piano.

As with the letter "A," we're not expecting immediate comprehension and retention. We know that it's the beginning of a long road toward fluency and literacy, and a critical road at that. Now with music, you can pave the road in much the same way. Small moments of learning, repeated over time to make sense of the sounds, symbols, and eventually playing of notes.

One aspect of music we haven't spoken much about yet is singing. Chances are, you've been singing to your child from even before they were born. Music education had already begun, and you didn't even know it. Now we just need to connect those melodies with words, notes, notation, and, ultimately, playing an instrument.

You'll find that, just as with music, this will be a natural evolution, and you will be their instructor all along the way.

■ Try This at Home

Find the C Game

If you have a keyboard or piano, show your child how to find the C note (left of two black keys). Sing "C" to a simple tune (e.g., *Twinkle, Twinkle*'s first note). Let them press it and sing along. Praise their effort. This connects sound to instrument play.

■ Parent Takeaway

Dust off that unused instrument and make it part of playtime. Teaching one note, like "C", starts your child's musical journey with ease.

■ Chapter Recap

1. **Music Sticks Through Play**: Songs like the *ABC Song* use music's brain-boosting power to make learning fun and memorable, not a chore.
2. **Games Build Habits**: Turn music practice into games with praise, like singing the ABCs, to keep kids engaged without pressure.
3. **Everyday Music Matters**: Add singing, dancing, and instrument play to daily routines to build fluency naturally, like language learning.
4. **Progress, Not Perfection**: Focus on small steps, like *Star Wars*' filming schedule, to keep music learning motivating and fun.
5. **Music Is Like Letters**: Teach notes like "C" as you teach the letter "A," using simple associations to build literacy effortlessly.
6. **You're the First Teacher**: You can guide your child's musical journey through play, no expertise needed.

Conclusion

Your Next Steps as a Parent-Teacher

> *The songs you sing to your children become the lullabies they sing to their own.*
>
> —Unknown

Whether we listen to the science behind how our brains develop or simply pause to reflect on our own lifelong relationship with music, the conclusion is the same: music is profoundly human.

It reaches deep into our souls and expresses what words alone cannot. Beyond the old debate of innate talent versus learned skill, music transcends both. It adds a depth to our lives that is as mysterious as it is universal. So, the question is not if we should bring music into a child's life, but why wouldn't we?

Like language, music is a system that every child is capable of learning fluently, if we nurture it. A child can survive without learning to read or write, but few would argue that literacy is optional. I believe music deserves that same importance.

Children are born ready to use their auditory systems long before they take their first breath. Many parents have even seen infants instinctively move to the rhythm of a song. Science now confirms what we've observed for generations: newborns can perceive musical beats.

A 2023 study from the University of Amsterdam and the HUN-REN Research Centre for Natural Sciences in Hungary showed that this ability isn't learned, it's a built-in cognitive mechanism active from birth.

My hope for you, as a parent, is to recognize that your child's brain was designed to process music. Even more, I hope you see that you are their first and most influential music teacher. Whether you realize it or not, you're already shaping their musical world. You're, in essence, your child's DJ during the most important years of their life.

Every song you play and sing, every movie or show you choose, these become part of your child's musical DNA. You're creating their ultimate lifelong playlist. So yes, it might be time to pick a DJ name. Just saying.

Although I didn't grow up with music specifically, I had the fortune of growing up with Spanish-speaking parents and I absorbed Spanish through everyday conversations, not lessons.

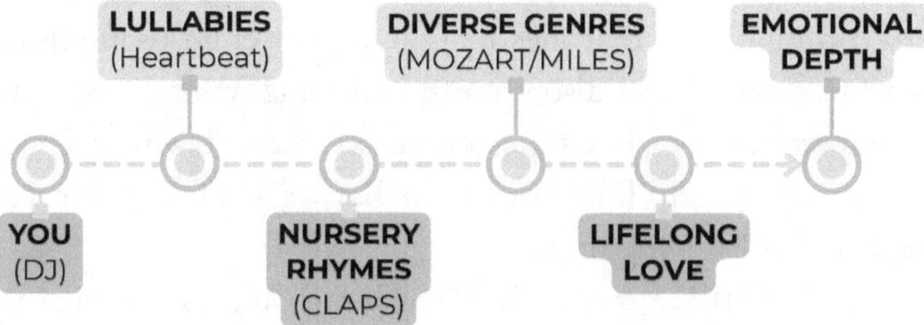

Music came much later, in high school, and it was then that I discovered its power. With my second language background and fluency, learning music felt natural and I absorbed it quicker than most at that age.

You can give your child an even richer musical start than I had, by curating a diverse soundtrack and musical richness that builds fluency and joy from day one.

■ Did You Know?

Newborns Detect Beats

A 2023 study confirmed that newborns perceive musical beats from birth, a cognitive mechanism that supports early rhythm and language development. Your baby is born musical! (Source: Winkler, I., *PNAS*).

What Will Your Child's First Musical Years Sound Like?

Let's continue with that idea of DJ'ing your child's soundtrack. It's a fun thought, but also a meaningful one. What if you pick the "wrong" music? Here's the good news: the only wrong choice is no music at all. That said, I do have a challenge for you: broaden your listening profile.

In *This Is What It Sounds Like*, Susan Rogers explores the concept of our unique "listening profiles", the patterns behind why we love the music we love. As she writes,

> *"Your record collection is a map of your emotional landscape."*

She explains that our preferences aren't random; they're built from emotional connections and familiar sonic experiences. As adults, we tend to stay within our musical comfort zones. We have our workout playlist, our chill playlist, and maybe one for family drives. But while that's fine for us, a child's developing brain needs variety.

Remember that Hungarian study about newborns and beat perception? It also highlights their statistical learning ability, the capacity to detect and internalize patterns from what they hear. That means early exposure to a wide range of music and sounds is essential.

I know that much of children's entertainment today is created to be catchy and fun (and that's okay), but not all of it expands their musical vocabulary. To put it another way, imagine only ever watching sitcoms. It might be enjoyable, but what would your imagination or emotional depth look like without novels, classic films, or paintings by Rembrandt?

When it comes to language, we speak to babies in real words from day one. We don't limit them to baby gibberish forever. We should treat music the same way. Yes, let them enjoy playful children's tunes, but also share with them the rich world of Mozart, Miles Davis, and Billie Holiday. They will absorb it, I promise you. I can say that now not just from intuition, but from science. Study after study confirms that babies and toddlers respond to, and learn from, complex musical patterns and rhythms. And they will have the coolest musical tastes ever.

■ Try This at Home

DJ Playlist Challenge

Create a weekly playlist with one new genre (e.g., classical, jazz, world music). Play it during dinner or playtime. Ask your child, "What does this sound like?" Dance or sing along. This broadens their musical world joyfully.

■ Parent Takeaway

You're your child's DJ, curate a diverse soundtrack. Variety now builds a richer musical brain for life.

Your Final Homework

SMALL STEPS. BIG LEGACY.*

- ☐ *Sing daily (lullabies, rhymes)*
- ☐ *Move together (dance, clap)*
- ☐ *Explore sounds (pots, xylophone)*
- ☐ *Praise every try*
- ☐ *Add variety (one new genre/week)*

**Your joyful homework, forever.*

Because long after they forget their favorite cartoon or toy, the soundtrack you created together will stay in their hearts. You've got this. From the first lullaby to the first note on a xylophone, you're building something beautiful. I created Color Me Mozart to guide you, but trust your instincts, you're already their perfect music teacher. Keep playing, keep praising, and watch your child's musical world bloom.

Thank you for joining me on this journey in *The First Music Teacher*. Your child's musical story starts with you—make it unforgettable.

■ Did You Know?

Variety Shapes Lifelong Preferences
Diverse early exposure builds emotional intelligence and creativity (Rogers & Ogas, 2022). Your playlist lasts forever!

■ Try This at Home

Family Soundtrack Night
Pick a theme (e.g., "happy songs") and take turns adding tracks to a shared playlist. Play it during a family activity. This makes music a bonding ritual.

■ Parent Takeaway

Music is your child's lifelong companion. Fill their early years with sound, and you're giving them a gift that echoes forever.

■ Chapter Recap (and Book Recap)

1. **Music Is Human**: It's universal, profound, and essential, like language literacy, it's not optional for a full life.
2. **You're the First Teacher**: From birth, you shape your child's musical DNA as their DJ, no expertise needed.
3. **Variety Is Key**: Broaden your playlist with complex genres to build a rich musical vocabulary, just as you use real words.
4. **Science Backs It**: Newborns detect beats; early exposure to diverse music fosters fluency and emotional depth.
5. **Play and Praise**: Make music daily through games, singing, and movement—turn practice into joyful habits.
6. **Your Legacy**: The soundtrack you create now will stay in your child's heart forever. Start with a music program such as Color Me Mozart and most importantly, keep going.

Appendix

Resources and Activities

10 Songs Every Parent Should Sing

(and why they're pure magic for little brains and big hearts)

1. **Itsy Bitsy Spider**
   The ultimate finger-play song. Those tiny hand motions help wire coordination, sequencing, and storytelling — plus kids beg for "again!"
2. **The Hokey Pokey**
   Left/right awareness, body-part vocabulary, and listening skills, all wrapped in giggles.
   Bonus: it teaches them to laugh at themselves early.
3. **If You're Happy and You Know It**
   Emotional literacy in action. Swap in "angry ➡ stomp feet," "silly ➡ wiggle nose," or "loved ➡ hug Mommy." They learn feelings have sounds and movements.
4. **Head, Shoulders, Knees, and Toes**
   Fast or super-slow, this song builds body awareness

and lightning-fast auditory processing. Speed it up each round and watch them beam with pride.

5. **The Wheels on the Bus**
   Endless verses = instant creativity. Let your child invent new ones ("The babies on the bus go wah-wah-wah!"). Call-and-response gold.
6. **Row, Row, Row Your Boat**
   Perfect first round/canon. Start together, then you begin again while they're still singing — their first taste of harmony and overlapping sound.
7. **Twinkle, Twinkle, Little Star**
   Same melody as the ABCs and "Baa Baa Black Sheep." One tune, three lifelong lessons. Also your go-to lullaby in any key, any tempo.
8. **Old MacDonald Had a Band** (not farm!)
   Swap animals for instruments: "Old MacDonald had a band, E-I-E-I-O... and on that band he had a drum!" Kids invent sounds and learn instrument names.
9. **This Is the Way** (morning routine song)
   "This is the way we brush our teeth, wash our face, put on shoes..." Turns chores into music and plants rhythm into daily life.
10. **You Are My Sunshine**
    The ultimate love song from parent to child. Sing it soft at bedtime, loud in the car, or silly with wrong words. They'll carry these lyrics in their heart forever.

(Print this list, stick it on the fridge, and watch the magic happen.)

Sing these ten songs on repeat for the first five years and your child will have rhythm, pitch, vocabulary, emotional awareness, and a treasure chest of memories, all before they ever touch an instrument.

Your voice + these songs = their first music lessons.

No curriculum required. Just love.

Music Activity Calendar

YOUR FAMILY'S FIRST 30 DAYS OF MUSIC PLAY

> *"One small moment a day… a lifetime of music in their heart."*

WEEK 1

Day 1 Sing "Itsy Bitsy Spider" with full hand motions during bath time

Day 2 Freeze Dance, pause the music and strike silly poses

Day 3 Kitchen Band, pots, spoons, and shakers. Record your hit single!

Day 4 Echo Game, you sing a 3-note phrase, child echoes (la-la-loo!)

Day 5 "If You're Happy and You Know It", make up new verses (hop, spin, roar!)

Day 6 Play a lullaby you loved as a child, tell them why it's special

Day 7 Find the C's on any keyboard/piano together (left of the two black keys)

WEEK 2

Day 8 Call-and-Response names: sing your child's name, they sing yours back
Day 9 Sound Safari: hunt 5 household "instruments" and name their sounds
Day 10 Dance Party: one song, everyone chooses one goofy move
Day 11 Sing the ABCs with claps on every letter
Day 12 "Wheels on the Bus": act out every verse (beep beep, swish swish)
Day 13 Genre Night: play jazz at dinner and guess the instruments
Day 14 Progress Jar: drop a bead every time you make music today

WEEK 3

Day 15 Make up a song about today's adventure (going to the park, eating pancakes...)
Day 16 Slow-motion "Head, Shoulders, Knees, and Toes"
Day 17 Play Mary Had a Little Lamb using only color stickers (free set at ColorMeMozart.com)
Day 18 Whisper-sing a favorite song, then loud-sing it!
Day 19 Mirror Song Game: copy each other's silly melodies

Day 20 Classical breakfast: play Vivaldi or Mozart while eating cereal

Day 21 Family band rehearsal: everyone picks an instrument (or body percussion)

WEEK 4

Day 22 "This Is the Way We…": make up new verses while brushing teeth

Day 23 Sound Story: read a book and add sound effects together

Day 24 Rhythm Echo: you clap a pattern, child copies, then leads

Day 25 Lullaby remix: sing Twinkle backwards or super slow

Day 26 World music night: one song from another country (salsa, bossa nova, reggae…)

Day 27 Trace the treble clef together (free worksheet at ColorMeMozart.com/worksheets)

Day 28 Celebrate! Count the beads in your Progress Jar and have a dance party

WEEK 5

Day 29 Sing your child's favorite song from the month — record it

Day 30 Start again… because music never ends ♫

Downloadable Resources

> *"The only wrong day is a silent one."*
> *— Your child's first music teacher (that's you)*

Keep the music going long after you close this book.

Scan the QR code or visit TheFirstMusicTeacher.com for every activity in this book, plus free color stickers, worksheets, playlists, and new ideas every month.

Your musical adventure starts here.

Acknowledgements

When I first set out to write this book, my first thought was that it would be a more daunting task than I could imagine. While that proved to be true, I was fortunately surrounded by an incredible group of people who always encouraged me to push beyond my comfort zone.

First and foremost, I want to thank my wife, Maria Alejandra, who has had to sit through more conversations about xylophones and neuroscience than anyone should have to in one lifetime. Yet she always listened, gave valuable feedback, and encouraged me to keep going with each passing page. Thank you for joining me on every new adventure that life gives us.

Secondly, I am grateful to my family, my mom and dad, and my two sisters, for being such a creative and loving foundation that always saw the importance of being yourself. A special thank you to my sister Adriana (yes, our parents decided we should have similar names) for always reminding me that dreaming big is always worth it, and that instead of losing yourself in your dreams, you actually discover who you were really meant to be.

Thirdly, I'm deeply grateful to the circle of friends who have inspired me, both directly and indirectly, over the years. In any creative journey, there are stretches when everything flows easily and others when momentum stalls completely. It's in those quiet, difficult moments that the people around you matter most: a timely word of encouragement, a shared laugh, or simply their steady presence can be the difference between giving up and pressing on. To every friend who lifted me when I needed it, a special thank you that goes beyond words, you know who you are.

A heartfelt thank you goes to the hundreds of students and families I've had, and continue to have, the privilege of serving through music. You are the true heartbeat of this journey. Watching you grow in confidence, joy, and musical expression has been one of the greatest rewards of my life as a musician and educator. Your curiosity, breakthroughs, and shared laughter have inspired every page of this book. Thank you for trusting me to be part of your story.

I'd also like to thank the many teachers, musicians, and academics who have inspired me for so many years, not just to pursue music as a career, but to explore why it holds such profound power in our lives and minds.

A special thank you to my college piano professor, Gary Hammond, for his belief in me as a young musician and for igniting a deeper love for music, and to Dr. Denise Young for her lifelong friendship and endless encouragement to do the hard things in life.

I'm also deeply grateful to the authors and musicians whose work shaped this book, including Dr. Susan Rogers, Dr. Edward Large, Dr. Daniel Levitin, Dr. Oliver Sacks, Isabelle Hau, and Victor Wooten.

And finally, to you, reading this book.

One of the things that brings me the greatest joy in life is being able to share the love of learning. Thank you for taking the time to read my thoughts and ideas. My hope is that you walk away with a deep love for music and all that it can bring to your family.

Notes

Chapter 1: SMASH THE MYTH

24 Williams, K. E., Barrett, M. S., McFerran, K. S., Vanderwert, R. E., & Mills, D. L. (2015). Five-year-olds' associations of musical emotion with facial expressions: The impact of musical training and associations with social and emotional development. *Music Science, 1*, 2059204315619967. https://doi.org/10.1177/2059204315619967

28 Rabinowitch, T.-C., Cross, I., & Burnard, P. (2013). Long-term musical group interaction has a positive influence on empathy in children. *Psychology of Music, 41*(4), 484–498. https://journals.sagepub.com/doi/abs/10.1177/0305735612440609

Chapter 2: YOU ALREADY HAVE WHAT IT TAKES

36 Rogers, S., & Ogas, O. (2022). *This is what it sounds like: What the music you love says about you*. W. W. Norton & Company.

40 Wooten, V. (2006). The music lesson: A spiritual search for growth through music. Berkley Books.

41 Sacks, O. (2007). *Musicophilia: Tales of music and the brain*. Alfred A. Knopf.

42 Hepper, P. G., Scott, D., & Shahidullah, S. (2014). Newborn and fetal response to maternal voice. *Journal of Reproductive and Infant Psychology, 11*(1), 147–153. https://doi.org/10.1080/02646839308403210

44 Hannon, E. E., & Trehub, S. E. (2019). Infant music perception: Domain-general or domain-specific mechanisms? *Developmental Science, 22*(3), e12772. https://doi.org/10.1111/desc.12772

44 Kirschner, S., & Tomasello, M. (2016). Joint music making promotes prosocial behavior in 4-year-old children. *Evolution and Human Behavior, 31*(5), 354–364. https://doi.org/10.1016/j.evolhumbehav.2010.04.004

45 Gordon, R. L., Shivers, C. M., Wieland, E. A., Kotz, S. A., Yoder, P. J., & McAuley, J. D. (2014). Musical rhythm discrimination explains individual differences in grammar skills in children. *Developmental Science, 18*(4), 635–642. https://doi.org/10.1111/desc.12238

Chapter 3: THE REAL PURPOSE OF MUSIC EDUCATION

57 Dehaene, S., Cohen, L., Morais, J., & Kolinsky, R. (2020). Illiterate to literate: Behavioural and cerebral changes induced by reading acquisition. *Nature Reviews Neuroscience, 21*(8), 427–438. https://doi.org/10.1038/s41583-020-0333-8

59 Kirschner, S., & Ilari, B. (2021). Joint drumming leads to communal prosocial behavior in preschool children. *Music Perception, 38*(3), 252–263. https://doi.org/10.1525/mp.2021.38.3.252

62 Williams, K. E., Barrett, M. S., Welch, G. F., Abad, V., & Broughton, M. (2018). Associations between early shared music activities in the home and later child outcomes: Findings from the Longitudinal Study of Australian Children. *Journal of Research in Music Education, 66*(3), 303–323. https://doi.org/10.1177/0022429418783685

65 Zatorre, R. J. (2016). Musical pleasure and reward: Mechanisms of superior temporal cortex activation. *Frontiers in Neuroscience, 10*, Article 571. https://doi.org/10.3389/fnins.2016.00571

Chapter 4: WHAT GETS IN THE WAY

68 Hallam, S. (2020). The power of music: Its impact on the intellectual, social and personal development of children and young people. *Psychology of Music, 48*(1), 3–19. https://doi.org/10.1177/0255761410370658

72 Hannon, E. E., Lévêque, Y., Nave, K. M., & Trehub, S. E. (2019). Infants' sensitivity to nonadjacent dependencies across native and non-native rhythms. *Journal of Experimental Child Psychology, 178*, 124–138. https://doi.org/10.1016/j.jecp.2018.09.009

74 Moser, J. S., Schroder, H. S., Heeter, C., Moran, T. P., & Lee, Y.H. (2017). Mind your errors: Evidence for a neural mechanism linking growth mindset to adaptive posterror adjustments.

Nature Communications, 8(1), Article 1253. https://doi.org/10.1038/s41467-017-01332-2

Chapter 5: SOUND IS THE FIRST INSTRUMENT

76 Gordon, R. L., Jacobs, M. S., Schuele, C. M., & McAuley, J. D. (2019). The babble boot camp: Effects of rhythm training on speech perception in infants. *Journal of Music, Technology & Education, 12*(1), 7–27. https://doi.org/10.1386/jmte_00001_1

79 Kraus, N., & White-Schwoch, T. (2021). The argument for music education. *Trends in Cognitive Sciences, 25*(5), 355–356. https://doi.org/10.1016/j.tics.2021.02.001

82 Partanen, E., Kujala, T., Näätänen, R., Liitola, A., Sambeth, A., & Huotilainen, M. (2013). Learning-induced neural plasticity of speech processing before birth. *Proceedings of the National Academy of Sciences, 110*(37), 15145–15150. https://doi.org/10.1073/pnas.1302159110

83 Rogers, S., & Ogas, O. (2022). *This is what it sounds like: What the music you love says about you*. W. W. Norton & Company.

85 Sacks, O. (2007). *Musicophilia: Tales of music and the brain*. Alfred A. Knopf.

Chapter 6: SINGING, SPEAKING, AND MUSICAL IMITATION

87 Feldman, R. (2020). Parent-infant synchrony: A biobehavioral model of mutual influences in the formation of affiliative bonds. *Developmental Cognitive Neuroscience, 41*, 100739. https://doi.org/10.1016/j.dcn.2019.100739

89 Gerry, D., Unrau, A., & Trainor, L. J. (2016). Active music classes in infancy enhance musical, language and social-emotional skills. *Developmental Science, 19*(5), 797–811. https://doi.org/10.1111/desc.12430

90 Jacobsen, J. H., Stelzer, J., Fritz, T. H., Chételat, G., La Joie, R., & Turner, R. (2017). Why musical memory can be preserved in advanced Alzheimer's disease. *NeuroImage, 153*, 108–118. https://doi.org/10.1016/j.neuroimage.2017.03.055

93 Williams, K. E., Barrett, M. S., Welch, G. F., Abad, V., & Broughton, M. (2018). Associations between early shared music activities in the home and later child outcomes: Findings from the Longitudinal Study of Australian Children. *Journal of Research in Music Education, 66*(3), 303–323. https://doi.org/10.1177/0022429418783685

Chapter 7: RHYTHM AND ROUTINE AS YOUR CURRICULUM

95 Gordon, R. L., Cordeaux, C., & Magne, C. L. (2020). Rhythm and reading: The role of musical training in phonological awareness. *Journal of Music, Technology & Education, 13*(2), 123–139. https://doi.org/10.1386/jmte_00019_1

98 Hannon, E. E., Lévêque, Y., Nave, K. M., & Trehub, S. E. (2019). Infants' sensitivity to nonadjacent dependencies across native and non-native rhythms. *Journal of Experimental Child Psychology, 178*, 124–138. https://doi.org/10.1016/j.jecp.2018.09.009

102 Levitin, D. J. (2006). *This is your brain on music: The science of a human obsession*. Dutton.

104 Menon, V., & Levitin, D. J. (2018). The rewards of music listening: Response and physiological connectivity of the mesolimbic system. *Journal of Cognitive Neuroscience, 30*(10), 1477–1492. https://doi.org/10.1162/jocn_a_01313

106 Rogers, S., & Ogas, O. (2022). *This is what it sounds like: What the music you love says about you*. W. W. Norton & Company.

109 Trainor, L. J., Marie, C., Gerry, D., Whiskin, E., & Unrau, A. (2016). Experience with music in infancy enhances musical and linguistic processing. *Developmental Science, 19*(5), 766–779. https://doi.org/10.1111/desc.12435

Chapter 8: MUSIC FLUENCY VS. MUSIC RECITATION

111 Goswami, U. (2017). A neural basis for phonemic awareness? A review of imaging and behavioral studies. *Child Development, 88*(1), 14–24. https://doi.org/10.1111/cdev.12666

113 Hallam, S. (2016). The impact of making music on aural perception, musical development and literacy. *Psychology of Music, 44*(3), 463–477. https://doi.org/10.1177/0305735615581465

114 Sowden, P. T., Clements, L., Redlich, C., & Lewis, C. (2019). Improvisation facilitates divergent thinking and creativity: Realizing the potential of script theory in the psychological sciences. *Psychology of Music, 47*(3), 323–341. https://doi.org/10.1177/0305735618816348

115 Stewart, L., Walsh, V., Frith, U., & Rothwell, J. (2020). Reading music and words: The neural bases of literacy in music and language. *Music Perception, 37*(5), 411–425. https://doi.org/10.1525/mp.2020.37.5.411

Chapter 9: THE ABCs OF MUSIC

117 Dzulkifli, M. A., & Mustafar, M. F. (2018). The influence of colour on memory performance: A review. *Procedia - Social and Behavioral Sciences, 222*, 812–818. https://doi.org/10.1016/j.sbspro.2018.01.118

118 Kirschner, S., & Ilari, B. (2021). Joint drumming leads to communal prosocial behavior in preschool children. *Music Perception, 38*(3), 252–263. https://doi.org/10.1525/mp.2021.38.3.252

120 Pyle, A., DeLuca, C., & Danniels, E. (2020). The influence of play-based learning on children's early literacy and numeracy skills. *Early Childhood Research Quarterly, 52*, 1–12. https://doi.org/10.1016/j.ecrq.2019.12.005

Chapter 10: MUSIC AS FAMILY GLUE

168 Isabelle C. Hau, Love to Learn: The Transformative Power of Care and Connection in Early Education (PublicAffairs, 2025), 234.

Chapter 11: TURNING PLAY INTO PRACTICE

130 Ferreri, L., Mas-Herrero, E., Zatorre, R. J., Ripollés, P., Gomez Andres, A., Alicart, H., Olivé, G., Marco-Pallarés, J., Antonijoan, R. M., Valle, M., Riba, J., & Rodriguez-Fornells, A. (2019). Dopamine modulates the reward experiences elicited by music. *Frontiers in Psychology, 10*, Article 132. https://doi.org/10.3389/fpsyg.2019.00132

170 McPherson, G. E., & Renwick, J. M. (2018). Self-regulation and mastery of musical skills. *Journal of Research in Music Education, 66*(1), 3–21. https://doi.org/10.1177/0022429418755682

172 Patel, A. D. (2017). Music, language, and the brain: An overview. In *Oxford handbook of music psychology* (2nd ed., pp. 1–18). Oxford University Press.

180 Pyle, A., DeLuca, C., & Danniels, E. (2020). The influence of play-based learning on children's early literacy and numeracy skills. *Early Childhood Research Quarterly, 52*, 1–12. https://doi.org/10.1016/j.ecrq.2019.12.005

Chapter 12: YOUR NEXT STEPS AS A PARENT-TEACHER

160 Honing, H., Bouchet, H., Hagoort, P., & Winkler, I. (2023). Newborn infants detect the beat in music. *Cognition, 241*, Article 105670. https://doi.org/10.1016/j.cognition.2023.105670

170 Rogers, S., & Ogas, O. (2022). *This is what it sounds like: What the music you love says about you*. W. W. Norton & Company.

About the Author

Adrian Edward is a musician, educator, author, and creator of Color Me Mozart, a parent-led music education program that helps families raise musical children without pressure, private lessons, or prior musical experience.

Born in Buenos Aires and raised in Brooklyn, New York, Adrian grew up bilingual in Spanish and English, absorbing language through everyday immersion long before any formal lessons. That same natural, ear-first process later shaped his own path into music. What began as curiosity became a lifelong passion for both performing and teaching.

As a musician and preschool educator, Adrian spent years watching young children light up when music was presented as play rather than performance. He founded Color Me Mozart to give parents the simple, science-backed tools to do the same at home, turning lullabies, kitchen rhythms, and silly songs into the foundation of musical fluency and literacy.

Adrian lives with his wife, Maria Alejandra, in beautiful North Carolina.

www.ingramcontent.com/pod-product-compliance
Lightning Source LLC
LaVergne TN
LVHW090512110826
845146LV00003B/826